Electoral Realignments

The Institution for Social and
Policy Studies at Yale University

THE YALE ISPS SERIES

Electoral Realignments

A CRITIQUE OF AN AMERICAN GENRE

David R. Mayhew

Yale University Press
New Haven & London

Designed by James J. Johnson and set in Aster Roman type by
Keystone Typesetting, Inc.
Printed in the United States of America by Vail-Ballou Press,
Binghamton, New York.

Library of Congress Cataloging-in-Publication Data

Mayhew, David R.
    Electoral realignments : a critique of an American genre / David R.
Mayhew.
        p. cm. — (The Yale ISPS series)
    Includes bibliographical references and index.
    ISBN 0-300-09336-5

    1. Political parties—United States—History. 2. Elections—United States—
History. 3. Party affiliation—United States—History. I. Title. II. Series.

JK2261 .M364 2002
324'.0973—dc21   2002016746

A catalogue record for this book is available from the British Library.

The paper in this book meets the guidelines for permanence and durability
of the Committee on Production Guidelines for Book Longevity of the
Council on Library Resources.

10 9 8 7 6 5 4 3 2 1

Contents

Acknowledgments

Many people helped me with this project. For their critical readings of the manuscript at various stages, I am grateful to Bruce Ackerman, Paul Allen Beck, Nigel Bowles, Robert Dahl, Alan Gerber, Donald Green, Jacob Hacker, Rogan Kersh, Joseph LaPalombara, Harvey Schantz, Eric Schickler, and Rogers Smith. For their comments following a presentation of the project at Yale University, I thank David Cameron and Stephen Skowronek. For comments provoked by a presentation of the project at a conference on American political development at the Massachusetts Institute of Technology, I am indebted to Richard Bensel, Walter Dean Burnham, Charles Cameron, John Gerring, David Hart, Christopher Howard, William Keech, Dan Kryder, and Martin Shefter. Important encouragement came from John Covell, Charles Lindblom, Byron Shafer, and Ian Shapiro. Useful tips on sources came from Ron Johnston, John Lapinski, Michael Layton, and Eric Patashnik. A major injection of accuracy came from Matthew Green, who checked the references. For books and articles, I drew on the libraries at Boston College, Boston University, Oxford University, and Yale University.

Introduction

1 THE STUDY OF AMERICAN ELECTORAL realignments, which enjoyed its heyday in the 1960s and 1970s, has been one of the most creative, engaging, and influential intellectual enterprises ever undertaken by American political scientists. During the 1960s and 1970s, it rivaled the Michigan election studies. Then and since, it has offered certifiable science, in the sense of a conceptual scheme, a theory, and quantitative analysis; breadth, in its tackling of large questions concerning the what, when, and why of American history; and even a secular eschatology, in the sense that it has encouraged generations of students and others, primed to seek "signs" along a presumed highway to an extraordinary historical destination, to keep asking: Is an electoral realignment about to happen? Are

we witnessing an electoral realignment this year? In the now familiar mode, a *New York Times* op-ed piece toyed with the idea during the 2000 election season, and a *Nation* article of that season bore the title "Whole Lotta Shakin' Goin' On: A Political Realignment Is on the Way."[1]

Basic to the appeal and influence of the realignments enterprise have been the talents of four major political scientists during its creative early days: the late V. O. Key, Jr., and E. E. Schattschneider, both of whom contributed important groundwork; and James L. Sundquist and Walter Dean Burnham, who provided the principal statements in the genre. All four of these writers exhibited a prodigious, sure-footed command of the factual particulars of American political history as well as the rare ability to generalize through detecting patterns. All four offered a kind of ideological excitement, as many academics of my generation will attest. It is small wonder that the genre made such a mark during its classical phase.

Inventive additions were made to the realignments interpretation in the 1970s and 1980s by, among others,

1. David M. Kennedy, "Bill Clinton in the Eye of History," *New York Times*, Nov. 2, 2000, A31. Walter Dean Burnham, "Whole Lotta Shakin' Goin' On: A Political Realignment Is on the Way," *The Nation*, Apr. 17, 2000, 11–15. A few months after the 2000 election, it was reported that George W. Bush's operative Karl Rove "continues to hold out the possibility that 2000 was a 'realigning election.'" See Stuart Rothenberg, "Throwing Cold Water on Rove's Vision of Political Realignment," *Roll Call*, March 1, 2001, online. See also David Frum, "We're on the Edge of Realignment," *American Enterprise* 12:2 (March 2001), 29–30.

the political scientists Paul Allen Beck, David W. Brady, and, writing as a threesome, Jerome M. Clubb, William H. Flanigan, and Nancy H. Zingale. In general, however, as is customary with academic schools, the creativity of the realignments genre tailed off after an initial phase. Trenchant critiques appeared.[2] The historians Richard L. McCormick and Joel H. Silbey, reflecting the sensibilities of their own discipline, offered periodizations of American political history that jarred against that of the realignments canon.[3] In the canon proper, there was little creativity in the 1990s.

Yet the realignments perspective lives on, at least in political science. In undergraduate courses on parties and elections, nothing has replaced it as a device for organizing

2. See, e.g., Allan J. Lichtman, "The End of Realignment Theory? Toward a New Research Program for American Political History," *Historical Methods* 15 (1982), 170–88; Richard L. McCormick, "The Realignment Synthesis in American History," *Journal of Interdisciplinary History* 13 (1982), 85–105; Richard L. McCormick, "Walter Dean Burnham and 'The System of 1896,'" *Social Science History* 10 (1986), 245–62; Peter H. Argersinger and John W. Jeffries, "American Electoral History: Party Systems and Voting Behavior," *Research in Micropolitics* 1 (1986), 1–33; Edward G. Carmines and James A. Stimson, *Issue Evolution: Race and the Transformation of American Politics* (Princeton: Princeton University Press, 1989), 19–26; Everett Carll Ladd, "Like Waiting for Godot: The Uselessness of 'Realignment' for Understanding Change in Contemporary American Politics," ch. 2 in Byron E. Shafer (ed.), *The End of Realignment? Interpreting American Electoral Eras* (Madison: University of Wisconsin Press, 1991).

3. Richard L. McCormick, "The Party Period and Public Policy: An Exploratory Hypothesis," *Journal of American History* 66 (1979), 279–98; Joel H. Silbey, "Beyond Realignment and Realignment Theory: American Political Eras, 1789–1989," ch. 1 in Shafer, *The End of Realignment*.

American political history. In conferences on American
political development, it is conventional wisdom. In academic journals, authors keep reaching for it as an authoritative framework.[4] In the minds of many political
scientists, notwithstanding the qualms of historians, the
two-century-long timetable associated with the realignments canon has come to have an unquestioned fixedness
approaching that of, I would imagine, the periodic table
for chemists. Also, "Whole Lotta Shakin'"–type statements in the popular media have become a trademark of
election seasons.

It is the continuing prominence of the realignments
genre that stirred me to write this work, which takes the
form of an empirical critique. It asks the question: How

4. See, e.g., John B. Gates, "The American Supreme Court and Electoral
Realignment," *Social Science History* 8 (1984), 267–90; David W. Brady, "A
Reevaluation of Realignments in American Politics: Evidence from the
House of Representatives," *American Political Science Review* 79 (1985), 28–
49; John B. Gates, "Partisan Realignment, Unconstitutional Policies, and
the U.S. Supreme Court, 1837–1964," *American Journal of Political Science*
31 (1987), 259–80; Peter F. Nardulli, "A Normal Vote Approach to Electoral
Change: Presidential Elections, 1828–1984," *Political Behavior* 16 (1994),
467–503; Peter F. Nardulli, "The Concept of a Critical Realignment, Electoral Behavior, and Political Change," *American Political Science Review* 89
(1995), 10–22; J. Mark Wrightson and Peverill Squire, "Uncontested Seats
and Electoral Competition for the U.S. House of Representatives over
Time," *Journal of Politics* 59 (1997), 452–68; Thomas L. Brunell and Bernard
Grofman, "Explaining Divided U.S. Senate Delegations, 1788–1996: A Realignment Approach," *American Political Science Review* 92 (1998), 391–99;
Daniel M. Shea, "The Passing of Realignment and the Advent of the 'Base-
less' Party System," *American Politics Quarterly* 27 (1999), 33–57; John H.
Aldrich, "Political Parties in a Critical Era," *American Politics Quarterly* 27
(1999), 9–32.

good is the realignments genre as a guide to the last two centuries of American electoral, party, and policy history? My answer: not very good at all—either in its classical version or since. Worse yet, I believe that the genre has evolved from a source of vibrant ideas into an impediment to understanding. In its current "normal science" form, it seems to be blinkering graduate students and exacting opportunity costs. For the political science discipline, in my view, it is time to move on. In this work, I do not try to advance any ambitious theory or conceptual scheme of my own—the work is a critique—but, in the large subject area commanded by the realignments genre, to open up lines of inquiry thought to be closed off is possibly by itself a kind of advance.

Chapter 2 is a nonjudgmental presentation of the essential claims, as I see them, of the realignments perspective. I begin by briefly taking up certain works by the four classical authors but then shift gears and present what might be considered a fully fleshed-out, maximally ambitious version of the realignments perspective—an ideal type about a scholarship already featuring ideal types. To do this is to lean heavily on Burnham, whose theoretical or empirical claims have been particularly ambitious; on Schattschneider, whose claims were equally ambitious if less completely worked out; somewhat less on Sundquist, who has been more cautious; and least of all on Key, whose claims were close to the vest. Also accommodated are the other political scientists noted above who made influential analytic moves during the 1970s and 1980s. There is a point in operating in this fashion: what I am calling the fully fleshed-out version of the realignments perspective has proven, I believe, to be particularly engaging and influential.

As an analytic technique, I resolve the large realignments perspective into fifteen distinct empirical claims. In Chapters 3 through 6, drawing on relevant primary and secondary sources where appropriate, I evaluate these fifteen claims for their empirical validity and illuminative power.[5] In Chapter 7, I close with some conclusions and a few points of more general interpretive criticism. In that chapter, as well as earlier, I point up what I am *not* doing in this work. I am not trying to argue that all American elections are equal. Unquestionably, some of them have been more engaging, momentous, or consequential in various ways than others. It is and should be a continuing scholarly task to illuminate such differences. Yet it is not helpful to get trapped forever in a failed model of illumination.

5. My approach in this work has some, albeit not all, of the characteristics of a meta-analysis.

The Realignments Perspective

2 WHAT IS THE ELECTORAL REALIGN-
ments perspective, and where did it come from?
As Harvey L. Schantz has noted, the idea of realigning elections surfaced in political science
before World War II.[1] Yet everyone agrees that it
was V. O. Key who crystallized and popularized the concept in his 1955 article "A Theory of Critical Elections."
Here we see the basic, trademark dichotomizing move
of the realignments school—the idea of sorting American presidential elections into two categories: a few that
are "critical elections," in Key's terminology, and a great

1. It appeared in the writings of Arthur N. Holcombe and Cortez A. M.
Ewing. See Harvey L. Schantz, "Realignment Before V. O. Key, Jr.," paper
presented at the annual convention of the Southern Political Science Association, Atlanta, October 28–31, 1998.

residual many that are not. The former are defined as ones "in which voters are, at least from impressionistic evidence, unusually deeply concerned, in which the extent of electoral involvement is relatively quite high, and in which the decisive results of the voting reveal a sharp alteration of the pre-existing cleavage within the electorate." Additionally, as "perhaps . . . the truly differentiating characteristic of this sort of election, the realignment made manifest in the voting in such elections seems to persist for several succeeding elections."[2]

Using data from townships in select New England states, Key identified the elections of 1896 (the showdown between Democrat William Jennings Bryan and Republican William McKinley) and of 1928 (the contest between Democrat Al Smith and Republican Herbert Hoover) as "critical elections" that brought notably sharp and long-lasting changes in voting patterns. That is all. Nothing appears in Key's foundational article about any critical elections prior to 1896, any possible periodicity in the occurrence of such elections, or any distinctive kinds of issue innovations or government policy results that might be associated with such elections. Also, Key seemed to back off critical elections somewhat four years later by highlighting patterns of "secular realignment"—that is,

2. V. O. Key, Jr., "A Theory of Critical Elections," *Journal of Politics* 17 (1955), 3–18, at 4.

gradual change—in voter coalitions.[3] Elsewhere in his writings, his comments on realignments are cautious and fleeting. Still, in 1955, thanks to Key, the idea of critical elections came to life.

E. E. Schattschneider weighed in with a quite different kind of contribution in 1956, which he reissued largely intact as the fifth chapter of his widely read *Semisovereign People* in 1960. Schattschneider's evocative framing of realignments was chatty rather than data-driven and was laden with far-reaching, if often elusive, empirical and theoretical claims rather than, as in Key's case, circumspect observations. Schattschneider zeroed in on the McKinley-Bryan election of 1896, "one of the decisive elections in American history," which, he asserted, brought on a party coalitional alignment "powerful enough to determine the nature of American politics for more than thirty years." The realignment of 1896 was "perhaps the best example in American history of the successful substitution of one conflict [that is, one cleavage between opposing clusters of interests] for another"—a signature Schattschneider

3. V. O. Key, Jr., "Secular Realignment and the Party System," *Journal of Politics* 21 (1959), 198–210. For a more recent statement on the idea of gradual as opposed to abrupt coalitional change, see Edward G. Carmines and James A. Stimson, "The Dynamics of Issue Evolution: The United States," ch. 5 in Russell J. Dalton, Scott C. Flanagan, and Paul Allen Beck (eds.), *Electoral Change in Advanced Industrial Democracies: Realignment or Dealignment?* (Princeton: Princeton University Press, 1984), 151–52.

concern. In turn, it took the later "revolution of 1932"—the election of Franklin Roosevelt—to "produce the greatest reversal of public policy in American history."[4]

Key and Schattschneider provided materials to build with. A half generation later, Sundquist presented a large, well-worked-out construction with his *Dynamics of the Party System*.[5] Probably most undergraduate students have learned about electoral realignments by way of this zestful, accessible volume that organizes so much of American political history so interestingly. Sundquist addresses realigning periods or eras rather than just single elections; he notes that a realignment "reaches its climax in one or more critical elections."[6] He dwells on three such eras that by around 1970 had become canonical: the 1850s, with its sectional crisis and Republican ascent to victory in 1860; the 1890s, with its Populist movement and McKinley-Bryan showdown; and the Depression-dogged 1930s. As with Schattschneider, the content of new voter cleavages—not just their statistical existence, as with

4. E. E. Schattschneider, "United States: The Functional Approach to Party Government," 194–215, in Sigmund Neumann (ed.), *Modern Political Parties: Approaches to Comparative Politics* (Chicago: University of Chicago Press, 1956); E. E. Schattschneider, *The Semisovereign People: A Realist's View of Democracy in America* (New York: Holt, Rinehart, and Winston, 1960), ch. 5, at 78, 81–82, 86.

5. James L. Sundquist, *Dynamics of the Party System: Alignment and Realignment of Political Parties in the United States* (Washington, D.C.: Brookings Institution, 1973; rev. ed., 1983).

6. Ibid. (1973), 294.

Key—is the signal feature associated with Sundquist's voter realignments. Yet in an updating touch appropriate to a new era of public opinion research, it is opposing issue positions, rather than, as in Schattschneider's case, opposing interests off which issue propensities could in principle unproblematically be read, that are said to index the cleavages. Sundquist is cautious. He is quick with a proposition or a generalization about behavior by voters or parties, but I could not pinpoint any claims in his work about, for example, the governmental policy consequences of realignments.

Of Burnham's many works on electoral realignments, three issued between 1965 and 1970 are perhaps the best guides to his thinking. In his seminal article "The Changing Shape of the American Political Universe," he associated the country's twentieth-century decline in voter turnout with the alleged electoral realignment of the mid-1890s.[7] In his chapter in the classic volume *The American Party Systems,* he organized American history into successive "party systems" bracketed by electoral realignments.[8] And in his *Critical Elections and the Mainsprings*

7. Walter D. Burnham, "The Changing Shape of the American Political Universe," *American Political Science Review* 59 (1965), 7–28.

8. Walter Dean Burnham, "Party Systems and the Political Process," ch. 10 in William N. Chambers and Burnham (eds.), *The American Party Systems: Stages of Political Development* (New York: Oxford University Press, 1967).

of American Politics, he provided his fullest statement.[9] Ample attention will be given to Burnham's specific claims below. In general, while embracing ideas set forth by Key and Schattschneider, Burnham went on to point the realignments scholarship toward additional instances of realigning elections, periodicity throughout American history, and policy effects said to be systematically associated with realignments. With these extensions, the realignments genre at the level of journal articles and graduate instruction became largely Burnham's.

Now for the shift of gears. A fully fleshed-out, maximally claim-laden version of the realignments perspective, I posit, can be sorted into a series of distinct claims about reality. Drawing on the relevant literature, I present fifteen such claims in this chapter. There is nothing magic about these particular fifteen; anyone else who happened to scrutinize the same literature would probably code it differently, though not radically so.[10] This empirical chunking may seem an odd way to proceed, but there is a reason for it. Any analyst approaching the realignments literature can get tied in knots over whether

9. Walter Dean Burnham, *Critical Elections and the Mainsprings of American Politics* (New York: Norton, 1970).

10. In an early, briefer version of this work, I listed only eleven such claims. See David R. Mayhew, "Electoral Realignments," *Annual Review of Political Science* 3 (2000), 449–74. I expanded the list to fifteen after rereading certain realignments works and reading ones that had escaped me before.

the features allegedly associated with realignments are causes, defining properties, concomitants, or consequences of them. I do not believe that those knots can be untied, and that to attempt a critique that is directly geared to the realignments canon's own conceptual structure would therefore be confusing and unproductive. Yet the canon's statements, regardless of what their place might be in any conceptual structure, can at least be probed for their truth value. That is my task here.

The fifteen claims are all in principle empirically testable, or at least they have a testable empirical side. All but the last are universalistic in form—at least across the domain of American national history. The last is historical. Taken together, claims 1 through 4 add up to the kind of content found in a cyclical theory of history—such as business-cycles theory. They feature a phenomenon that recurs, a specified periodicity of the recurrence, and two alternative causes of the alleged periodicity. (In this work, I tackle these causes by seeing if they leave the identifying tracks of evidence they are supposed to.) Claims 5 through 7 take up process events that are thought to map onto electoral realignments in various ways, claims 8 through 10 take up issue events, and claims 11 through 13 take up government policy events. Claims 14 and 15 are not easily classifiable.

Here are the fifteen claims:

1) *Through the examination of patterns of voter support for parties over time, American national elections can
be sorted into two kinds—a few specified realigning ones
and a great many nonrealigning ones.* This is the genre's
foundational empirical claim. The terminology can be
blurry: The terms *critical* and *realigning* have not been syn-
onymous for all authors. There is the messy matter of eras
as opposed to single elections: The election of 1860, which
triggered the Civil War, often sprawls back to encompass
most of the 1850s; the election of 1896 is often joined to
the sweeping Republican midterm victory of 1894; the
1928 and 1932 elections are variously treated as distinct
and unrelated events, related events, or part of the same
continuing event. For the most part, the literature addresses only presidential elections, but some authors take
up congressional ones. Still, Key's claim of 1955 has remained central: "Both sharp and durable" are the voter
alignment changes brought by some elections, but not by
others.[11] For Burnham, critical elections have differed
from all others "not in degree but in kind."[12] Sundquist is
less committed to a binary distinction in principle,[13] but
he dwells on the canonical realignments in practice. Con-
sensus has reigned in the genre on the requirement of

11. Key, "A Theory of Critical Elections," 11.
12. Burnham, "Party Systems and the Political Process," 287.
13. Sundquist, *Dynamics of the Party System* (1983), 8.

durability.[14] As for the elections in question: "There has long been agreement among historians that the elections of . . . 1800 [which brought Jefferson to power], 1828 [Jackson], 1860 [Lincoln], 1896 [McKinley], and 1932 [Franklin Roosevelt], for example, were fundamental turning points in the course of American electoral politics"[15]—a Burnham judgment in 1970 that has not drawn much dissent among political scientists.[16]

Strictly speaking, the reader may notice, this first claim can be sorted into two distinct subclaims: that the universe of American elections can be dichotomized *and* that the results of that dichotomization can be mapped onto specified time junctures. I am blending those two strands here, as the realignments literature usually does. In general, the same body of evidence is relevant to assessing both strands. Where appropriate, I will decouple the strands.

   2) *Electoral realignments have appeared in a pattern of*

14. Ibid., 4, 159; Burnham, "Party Systems and the Political Process," 288–89; Burnham, *Critical Elections and the Mainsprings*, 4–5.

15. Burnham, *Critical Elections and the Mainsprings*, 1.

16. An unchanged Burnham judgment in 1991: "In the United States all elections are equal, but some are decidedly more equal than others. It has been clear to modern American historians for fifty years or more that likely candidates for the latter category of elections are found in the years 1800, 1828, 1860, 1896, and 1932." Walter Dean Burnham, "Critical Realignment: Dead or Alive?" ch. 5 in Byron E. Shafer (ed.), *The End of Realignment? Interpreting American Electoral Eras* (Madison: University of Wisconsin Press, 1991), 101.

regularity—that is, periodicity. This claim is absent in Key, as noted earlier, but it is prominent in Burnham and available in qualified form in Sundquist.[17] For Burnham, who once wrote a chapter entitled "The Periodicity of American Critical Realignments,"[18] a realignment cycle emerges "approximately once every thirty years,"[19] or in another formulation "approximately once a generation, or every thirty to thirty-eight years." Also from Burnham: "Historically speaking, at least, national critical realignments have not occurred at random. Instead, there has been a remarkably uniform periodicity in their appearance." "This periodicity has had an objective existence." There has been a "periodic rhythm," a "cycle of oscillation."[20] From Paul Allen Beck: "Realignments have occurred at roughly three-decade intervals, and each realignment has been followed by a long period of stable normal politics."[21]

What has motored the American system through these cycles of such notable regularity? Two distinct theories address this question, one emerging around 1970 and the other a few years later. Since the theories are not contra-

17. See claim 4, below, for a discussion of Sundquist's view on this point.
18. Burnham, *Critical Elections and the Mainsprings*, ch. 2.
19. Burnham, "Party Systems and the Political Process," 288.
20. Burnham, *Critical Elections and the Mainsprings*, 26, 8, 181.
21. Paul Allen Beck, "A Socialization Theory of Partisan Realignment," ch. 10 in Richard G. Niemi and associates, *The Politics of Future Citizens* (San Francisco: Jossey-Bass, 1974), 207.

dictory, either or both might be taken to help the overall story along.

3) *First motor: A dynamic of tension buildup has caused the oscillation in and out of the thirty-year-or-so realignment cycles.* This is Burnham's thinking, with an assist from Sundquist. On this topic, the realignments genre has traveled on suggestions and metaphors rather than on sustained argument, but it has probably been no less influential for that, and the theory is worth teasing out. In brief, what happens in Burnham's account is that political "stress" or "tensions" build up following the last electoral realignment until they "escalate to a flash point" or a "boiling point," at which time a "triggering event" brings on a new realignment.[22] Notice the terms "flash point" and "boiling point" with their connotation, as in the Marxist dialectic, of a change in quantity being overtaken by a change in quality.

To put it more elaborately, there exists a "dynamic, even dialectic polarization between long-term inertia and concentrated bursts of change." Ordinarily, American institutions tend toward "underproduction of other than currently 'normal' policy outputs. They may tend persistently to ignore, and hence not to aggregate, emergent political demand of a mass character until a boiling point of

22. Burnham, *Critical Elections and the Mainsprings,* 4, 10, 27, 135, 136, 181.

some kind is reached." In another of Burnham's passages, "The socioeconomic system develops but the institutions of electoral politics and policy formation remain essentially unchanged." Consequently stacked up are "dislocations," "dysfunctions," and "increasingly visible social maladjustments," which are not sufficiently attended to until the political system catches up with a lurch as "incremental bargaining politics" gives way to "nonincremental change."[23] Sundquist, reflecting a view once popularized by reformers and Progressive historians, gives a corresponding cast to the politics of the latter part of the nineteenth century leading up to the mid-1890s. "Patronage, rather than program, became the object of politics." For twenty years, the party system was based on "dead issues of the past," offering voters "no means of expressing a choice on the crucial issues of domestic economic policy around which the country had been polarizing." Then, with the Democrats' nomination of Bryan in 1896, "the party system took on meaning once again. The day of political unresponsiveness, of evasion and straddling on fundamental, burning questions, was over."[24]

4) *Second motor: A strengthening and weakening of party identification has caused the oscillation in and out of the thirty-year-or-so realignment cycles.* Sundquist offered

23. Ibid., 27, 135, 137, 181.
24. Sundquist, *Dynamics of the Party System* (1973), 92–94, 144, at 93, 144.

this idea in 1973,[25] Beck crystallized and elaborated it in 1974,[26] and Burnham has since embraced it.[27] The passions and crisis atmosphere of a realignment juncture, the argument goes, bring on party identifications that are exceptionally strong. "For many people the emotional attachment to one party and the hostility toward the other formed at a time of crisis remain an essential part of their personal identities for the rest of their lives."[28] Strong identities of this kind freeze electoral behavior for quite a while. Yet as time goes on, more and more younger voters untransfixed by such realignment-induced identification come along. The socializing of children into parental party identities sags with each generation, eventually supplying voters who enjoy "little insulation from the short-term political forces they encounter as young adults." Accordingly, some twenty-five years after the last realignment, in Beck's view, the electorate is "ripe for realignment" once again. Put simply, "the prior disengagement of young voters from the established party system is a necessary precondition for realignment."[29]

But this disengagement is not a sufficient condition. In

25. Ibid., 33–36, 281–83. A slightly amended version appears in Sundquist (1983), 45–47, 304–6.

26. Beck, "A Socialization Theory of Party Realignment."

27. Burnham, "Critical Realignment: Dead or Alive?" 111.

28. Sundquist, *Dynamics of the Party System* (1973), 281.

29. Beck, "A Socialization Theory of Party Realignment," 207, 211, 212, 216.

Beck's terminology, an exogenously caused, possibly ran-
domly occurring "societal trauma" like the sectional conflict of the 1860s or the devastating depressions of the
1890s and 1930s is a necessary condition.[30] Thus the "ripeness" of the electorate may or may not usher in an electoral
realignment. Sundquist makes a similar contingent argument.[31] In effect, an interaction variable is in play here;
"ripeness" and "societal trauma" need to occur jointly
to cause the predicted effect. The traumas of the 1860s,
1890s, and 1930s could trigger realignments, yet in Beck's
account: "Other traumas of at least equal magnitude—the
economic depressions of 1873 and 1907, two world wars,
and the anticommunist hysteria of the early cold war period, for example—had no more than short-lived impacts
on partisan behavior."[32]

Again, these first four claims offer a dichotomizing
concept, periodicity, and two alternative versions of a
dynamic—the needed components of a cyclical theory.
Taken up in the next three claims are process events
that have figured in various theoretical roles as causes,
properties, indicators, concomitants, or precursors of realignments.

5) *Voter concern and turnout are unusually high in
realigning elections.* This idea goes back to Key, as noted

30. Ibid., 207, 212, 217, at 212.
31. Sundquist, *Dynamics of the Party System* (1973), 36.
32. Beck, "A Socialization Theory of Party Realignment," 212.

earlier,[33] and it is embraced by at least Burnham: "The rise in intensity is also normally to be found in abnormally heavy voter participation for the time."[34]

6) *Realignments are marked by turmoil in presidential nominating conventions.* The intensity surrounding critical elections, in Burnham's account, "typically spills over into the party nominating and platform-writing machinery during the upheaval and results in major shifts in convention behavior. . . . Ordinarily accepted 'rules of the game' are flouted; the party's processes, instead of performing their usual integrative functions, themselves contribute to polarization."[35]

7) *For one reason or another, good showings by third parties tend to stimulate, or at least to take place shortly before, realignments.* Emphasized in the genre are the Liberty party of 1844 and Free Soil party of 1848 that preceded the Civil War realignment; the Greenback party of the late 1870s and People's (Populist) party of 1892 that preceded the 1896 realignment; and the Progressive party candidacy of Robert La Follette of 1924 that preceded the New Deal realignment. No writer has posited a deterministic, one-to-one connection between third parties and realignments, but various logics conjure up a pattern of the former leading to the latter. For Sundquist, a third party

33. Key, "A Theory of Critical Elections," 4.
34. Burnham, *Critical Elections and the Mainsprings*, 7–8.
35. Ibid., 6–7.

may seize on a new explosive issue arising in society, attract a following, and go on to trigger an electoral realignment either by rising to major-party status itself or by enticing one of the major parties to adopt its cause.[36] As regards the 1890s and 1920s, an argument of this sort is cursorily presented by Key.[37] For Burnham, third-party movements of a "protest" variety, sometimes occurring as early as the midpoint of a "party system" as with the Greenbackers, figure as "protorealignment phenomena" in his model of tension buildup.[38] For Beck, a generation "ripe" for realignment by virtue of flagging party identification is especially likely to cast ballots for third parties.[39]

Next are the three claims about issues.

8) *In an electoral realignment, a new dominant voter cleavage over interests, ideological tendencies, or issues replaces an old one.* As noted earlier, this important claim is central to Schattschneider's and Sundquist's work, though not to Key's. I do not see it as a clear, upfront assertion in Burnham's. For Schattschneider, the 1896 realignment brought on a durable new "cleavage" or "conflict" as such groups as "southern conservative Democrats," "northern

---

36. Sundquist, *Dynamics of the Party System,* (1983), 28–32, 312–13.

37. V. O. Key, Jr., *Politics, Parties, and Pressure Groups* (New York: Thomas Y. Crowell, 5th ed., 1964), 257–58, 261–62, 280.

38. Burnham, *Critical Elections and the Mainsprings,* 27–29, at 27–28.

39. Beck, "A Socialization Theory of Party Realignment," 212; Paul Allen Beck, "The Electoral Cycle and Patterns of American Politics," *British Journal of Political Science* 9 (1979), 129–56, at 132–40.

conservatives," the "northern business-Republican minority," and "southern and western agrarian radicals" rearranged their alliances.[40] In a somewhat different argument, the 1932 realignment was "closely related to a profound change in the agenda of American politics" as a "sectional" cleavage gave way to a "national" one.[41] (Schattschneider does not point to any "agenda" change in his treatment of 1896, and he does not discuss any reworking of alliances among interests or ideological groupings in his treatment of 1932.) For Sundquist, a new "issue" or "cluster of related issues" can provoke and highlight a realignment, as did slavery in the 1850s and the questions of "what should the government do about the hardships of the farmers and about inequality in the distribution of wealth and income among regions and classes?" in the 1890s, and "what should the government do about the Great Depression?" in the 1930s.[42]

9) *Elections at realignment junctures are marked by insurgent-led ideological polarization.* This is a Burnham claim. It combines the idea of ideological style with the idea of polarization. "The rise in intensity [during realignments] is associated with a considerable increase in ideological polarizations, at first within one or more of the major parties and then between them. Issue distances

40. Schattschneider, *The Semisovereign People,* 78–82.
41. Ibid., 86–90.
42. Sundquist, *Dynamics of the Party System* (1983), 35, 298–99.

between the parties are markedly increased, and elections tend to involve highly salient issue-clusters, often with strongly emotional and symbolic overtones, far more than is customary in American electoral politics."[43] Also: "In the campaign or campaigns [during a realignment], the insurgents' political style is exceptionally ideological by American standards; this in turn produces a sense of grave threat among defenders of the established order, who in turn develop opposing ideological positions."[44]

10) *At least as regards the U.S. House, realigning elections hinge on national issues, nonrealigning elections on local ones.* This is a recent contribution by David W. Brady that I have not come across in any other scholarship. "Certain elections," he claims, "are dominated by national rather than local issues." Brady undertakes to demonstrate that "during realignments" the House is elected "on national, not local issues, thus giving a sense of mandate to the new majority party."[45]

Particularly important are the next three claims about government policy. Claim 12 overlaps claim 11, but their logics and factual structures differ.

43. Burnham, *Critical Elections and the Mainsprings*, 7.

44. Burnham, "Party Systems and the Political Process," 288.

45. David W. Brady, *Critical Elections and Congressional Policy Making* (Stanford: Stanford University Press, 1988), 14, 18.

11) *Electoral realignments are associated with major changes in government policy.* Recessive at best in Sundquist, this claim infuses both Schattschneider and Burnham, albeit complicatedly. For Schattschneider, the 1932 realignment obviously ushered in important changes in policy, and the voter alignment caused by the 1896 election no less obviously underpinned major policy results for a generation,[46] but did the 1896 election bring about *changes* in policy? That he stops short of asserting, not least, evidently, owing to his judgment that "aside from the protective tariff and the gold standard" the newly dominant Republicans of the McKinley era *"had no important positive program of legislation."* Catering to business interests trying to keep the government off their backs, the party gauged its policy success "in terms of *what was prevented"*—not in terms of what was initiated or enacted.[47] Burnham, in his more recent writings, has acknowledged this lack of post-1896 innovation: "Unlike the turnovers of 1828, 1860, or 1932, the realignment of 1894–1896 *did not* result in a major reversal of dominant public policy."[48]

Burnham, however, in the realignment genre's classic

46. Schattschneider, "United States: The Functional Approach to Party Government," 208, 205.

47. Ibid., 197–98; italics in the original in both cases.

48. Walter Dean Burnham, "Periodization Schemes and 'Party Systems': The 'System of 1896' as a Case in Point," *Social Science History* 10 (1986), 263–313, at 269; italics in original. See also Burnham, "The System of 1896: An Analysis," ch. 5 in Paul Kleppner et al., *The Evolution of American Electoral Systems* (Westport, Conn.: Greenwood, 1981), 175.

days, did not shrink from rendering bold, general, un-
asterisked assertions. A critical realignment constitutes "a
turning point in the mainstream of national policy formation."[49] Critical realignments "are intimately associated
with and followed by transformations in large clusters
of policy."[50] They "have been followed by significant alterations in national public policies."[51] They "result in
significant transformations in the general shape of policy."[52] A comment by Key approached these claims: critical electoral junctures like those of 1896 or 1928–36, he
remarked in the 1964 edition of his widely used text on
parties, "clear the way for a broad new direction in the
course of public policy."[53] Assertions like these have had a
life. Brady, in a recent work, takes it as given that the aftermaths of alleged realignments are times to canvass for
successful major policy innovations, examines the three
chief canonical aftermaths (although no other times),
and claims to detect such major innovations during those
aftermaths. Through overcoming "policy incrementalism," his reasoning goes, "realigning or critical elections
create conditions under which majorities are capable of

49. Burnham, "Party Systems and the Political Process," 289.

50. Burnham, *Critical Elections and the Mainsprings*, 9.

51. Walter Dean Burnham, "American Politics in the 1970's: Beyond
Party?" ch. 11 in William N. Chambers and Walter Dean Burnham (eds.),
The American Party Systems: Stages of Political Development (New York: Ox-
ford University Press, 2d ed., 1975), 310.

52. Burnham, *Critical Elections and the Mainsprings*, 10.

53. Key, *Politics, Parties, and Pressure Groups* (1964), 535.

legislating clusters of policy changes." "The Congresses of the Civil War, 1890's, and New Deal eras were responsible, in part, for outpourings of new comprehensive public policies."[54]

12) *Electoral realignments bring on long spans of unified party control of the government—that is, of the House, Senate, and presidency; such spans are a precondition of major policy innovation.* In the words of Clubb, Flanigan, and Zingale in 1980: "Consistent unified control of some duration by a single party is a significant condition for achieving major policy innovation."[55] Indeed, "the only rival circumstance seems to be an external military threat." Of such spans of party control, the uniquely long and important ones have been the fourteen-year stretches of Republican rule after 1860, Republican rule after 1896, and Democratic rule after 1932—all brought on by electoral realignments. Such longevity is crucial for policy making: it allows "time for program formation and development, for new policies to be assimilated by the populace

54. Brady, *Critical Elections and Congressional Policy Making,* vii, 4. See also 18.

55. Jerome M. Clubb, William H. Flanigan, and Nancy H. Zingale, *Partisan Realignment: Voters, Parties, and Government in American History* (Beverly Hills, Calif.: Sage, 1980), ch. 5, at 162. See also Walter D. Burnham, Jerome M. Clubb, and William H. Flanigan, "Partisan Realignment: A Systemic Perspective," ch. 1 in Joel H. Silbey, Allan G. Bogue, and William H. Flanigan (eds.), *The History of American Electoral Behavior* (Princeton: Princeton University Press, 1978), 64–70.

at large, to gain support, and to become embedded in the governmental and legal structures. Hence, the likelihood of reversal and dismantlement of policies and programs diminishes with the duration of control by the initiating party." On the record, as in claim 11 above, there has been policy payoff: "Impressionistic evidence clearly suggests that the partisan realignments of the Civil War years, the 1890s, and the 1930s were associated with major policy innovations."[56]

13) *Electoral realignments are distinctively associated with "redistributive" policies.* This is a relatively recent Burnham idea, building on Theodore J. Lowi's well-known three-category typology.[57] There is no reason to expect "distributive" or "regulatory" policy making to map onto realignment cycles in any predictable way, Burnham states or implies, but "matters become quite different when we turn to *redistributive* policies"—that is, initiatives of classwide impact such as Social Security. "Such policies are the heart of critical-realignment periods and are among the most important of their 'symptoms.'"[58]

Next to last is an exceptionally large claim that capstones and, to some degree, duplicates or incorporates

56. Clubb, Flanigan, and Zingale, *Partisan Realignment*, 157, 162–64, 185n3.

57. Theodore J. Lowi, "American Business, Public Policy, Case-Studies, and Political Theory," *World Politics* 16 (1964), 677–715.

58. Burnham, "Periodization Schemes and 'Party Systems,'" 270; italics in original.

most of the rest, but it is worth stating independently. It is at least an empirical claim, although other readings are possible.

14) *The American voting public expresses itself effectively and consequentially during electoral realignments, but not otherwise.* This is the heart of the realignments case. Note carefully the language used in assertions like this one from Burnham: "The voting public has made vitally important contributions to American political development approximately once in a generation."[59] That is, the public has done that at those junctures but not otherwise. From Key: "Elections that partake of this critical nature [that is, ones like 1896 and 1928–36] are the most striking instances of electoral interposition in the governing process."[60] For Sundquist, the public had "no means of expressing a choice on the crucial issues of domestic economic policy" for twenty years—a long time—but then in 1896 "the party system took on meaning once again."[61] For Schattschneider, the voter alignment brought on by the 1896 election "determined"—an unusually strong verb— "the nature of American politics from 1896 to 1932."[62]

59. Burnham, "Party Systems and the Political Process," 287.
60. Key, *Politics, Parties, and Pressure Groups* (1964), 535.
61. Sundquist, *Dynamics of the Party System* (1973), 144.
62. Schattschneider, "United States: The Functional Approach to Party Government," 201. In Schattschneider's formulation in *The Semisovereign People,* that realignment "was powerful enough to determine the nature of American politics for more than thirty years" (78).

That is, voters could not or did not do anything effective or consequential after that time for a third of a century.

Finally, the historical claim:

15) *There existed a "System of 1896."* This claim figures so prominently in the work of both Schattschneider and Burnham—it is something like a large container packed with its own content yet snugly insertable into the larger realignments vehicle—that it merits special mention. The "function" of the voter alignment struck by the McKinley-Bryan election of 1896, Schattschneider wrote, using an explanatory terminology in vogue in the 1950s, was to award political and economic supremacy to the American business class—a result that stuck for a "determined" thirty-six years. The Republican party, "the political instrument of business," ordinarily ruled during that time. The sectional shape of the post-1896 alignment—that is, the newly accentuated one-party rule by Democrats in the South and by Republicans in much of the North—was a key aspect of that hegemony: "Both sections became extremely conservative because one-party politics tends strongly to vest political power in the hands of people who already have economic power." In addition, "the sectional party alignment was unfavorable to the development and exploitation of new alternatives in public affairs."[63]

---

63. Schattschneider, "United States: The Functional Approach to Party Government," 197, 202, 205.

In the following statements Burnham has highlighted the American business sector's "insulation" from "mass pressures" after 1896. The 1896 alignment, in his view, "almost certainly" depressed voter turnout for a generation or more, notably through depositing noncompetitive one-partyism across both the North and the South. Accordingly, "the functional result of the 'system of 1896' was the conversion of a fairly democratic regime into a rather broadly based oligarchy." In 1965 he wrote that in general terms, "this [1896] realignment brought victory beyond expectation to those who had sought to find some way of insulating American elites from mass pressures."[64] In 1967: The "chief function" of the post-1896 party system was "the substantially complete insulation of elites from attacks by the victims of the industrializing process."[65] And in 1986: "I have no doubts that *in general* the system established in the 1890s was in fact a political matrix which insulated industrial and finance capital from adverse mass pressures for a generation afterward."[66]

Let no one underestimate the intellectual aspiration of these Schattschneider and Burnham claims about the

64. Burnham, "The Changing Shape of the American Political Universe," 23, 25.

65. Burnham, "Party Systems and the Political Process," 301.

66. Burnham, "Periodization Schemes and 'Party Systems,'" 269; italics in original. See also Burnham, "The System of 1896: An Analysis" (1981), 181.

System of 1896. There is an echo of Barrington Moore, Jr.:[67] "The take-off phase of industrialization has been a brutal and exploitative process everywhere, whether managed by capitalists or commissars. A vital functional political need during this phase [that is, during the late nineteenth and early twentieth centuries in the American case] is to provide adequate insulation of the industrializing elites from mass pressures."[68] There is an answer to the question: Why no socialism in the United States? "One is indeed inclined to suspect that the large hole in voter participation which developed after 1900 roughly corresponds to the area in the electorate where a viable socialist movement 'ought' to have developed."[69] And there is an answer to the question: Why no European-style welfare state in the United States? "The accomplishments of the [post-1896] Republican party might be measured more accurately, therefore, by the gap produced between the social legislation of western European countries and that of the United States before 1932."[70]

67. That is, of the dark interpretation of economic progress set forth in Barrington Moore, Jr., *Social Origins of Dictatorship and Democracy: Lord and Peasant in the Making of the Modern World* (Boston: Beacon Press, 1966).

68. Burnham, "The Changing Shape of the American Political Universe," 24.

69. Burnham, "Party Systems and the Political Process," 301. See also Burnham, "The System of 1896: An Analysis," 195.

70. Schattschneider, "United States: The Functional Approach to Party Government," 198.

Those are the fifteen claims. They add up to a grand, even magnificent interpretive structure—a view of how American political history has taken place. I hope that I have stayed true to the texts and that I have expressed fairly the ideas of the various authors.

Framing the Critique

3 HOW WELL DOES THE CLASSICAL RE-alignments genre stand up at the start of the twenty-first century, well past its base in histor-ical evidence and a generation or two beyond the main assertions by its chief exponents?

All the claims I have presented here can, in principle, be assessed for their empirical validity; that is the princi-pal task I undertake in the remainder of this work. How can this be done? In some instances, reasonably hard em-pirical information is available in published works and can be assembled. Yet in many instances that course is not possible, and one must resort to conventional wisdom that has been piled up by many generations of historians writing standard works about American political history— or at least that conventional wisdom as I apprehend it. For recent times, there is also my own experience of living under and witnessing the American regime. These are fallible reliances, yet what are the alternatives? It is not responsible, as the realignment writers would likely agree, simply to throw up one's hands when confronted by provocative assertions on large, important, not easily tractable matters.

A second concern, beyond validity, is the illuminative power of the realignments genre. What has been its value added? What would we be thinking about American electoral history otherwise? What did we think before the realignments genre came along? In this regard, it has always been obvious that certain American elections have surpassed others in engaging voters, generating a sense of high stakes among voters, shaking up received voter alignments, or spurring notable changes in government policy. Elections are not all equal. That is baseline knowledge. Certainly the election of 2000, to name one, was unusual. In addition, virtually everyone would agree that the Civil War and New Deal eras have stood out in American history for both their electoral turbulence and their policy innovations. That is baseline knowledge also. A plausible question is: What has the realignments genre added beyond these baselines?

Probably the chief contemporary charge against the realignments genre is that it has ceased to be relevant: No certifiable electoral realignment has occurred since 1932.

A sixty-eight-year gap obviously seems overly long for a theory of thirty-year-or-so electoral cycles, and at least three explanations have been offered for this embarrassment. Perhaps the decomposition of American parties in the 1960s and 1970s—the rise of ticket splitting and independent voter identities possibly brought on by new media technologies—sent the old realignments dynamic to the attic.[1] Perhaps the two major parties, hungry for victory as always yet better informed in an age when scientific surveys can pinpoint the median voter, have learned to steer clear of polarizing.[2] Finally, for Beck and Sundquist, an electoral realignment failed to occur on schedule in the 1960s and 1970s because, as their theories allow, that era lacked a strong enough triggering event—or at least one that impinged on the parties appropriately.[3]

Burnham, however, in a surprising move, argues that "there in fact *was* a critical realignment in the 1968–72 period. One of its essential features lay in the very dissolu-

1. See, e.g., Walter Dean Burnham, *Critical Elections and the Mainsprings of American Politics* (New York: Norton, 1970), ch. 5 ("The Contemporary Scene I: The Onward March of Party Decomposition"), 91–92; Martin P. Wattenberg, *The Decline of American Political Parties, 1952–1994* (Cambridge: Harvard University Press, 1996), chs. 1–3.

2. John G. Geer, "Critical Realignments and the Public Opinion Poll," *Journal of Politics* 53 (1991), 434–53.

3. Paul Allen Beck, "A Socialization Theory of Partisan Realignment," ch. 10 in Richard G. Niemi and associates (eds.), *The Politics of Future Citizens* (San Francisco: Jossey-Bass, 1974), 216; James L. Sundquist, *Dynamics of the Party System: Alignment and Realignment of Political Parties in the United States* (Washington, D.C.: Brookings Institution, 1983), ch. 17.

tion of the traditional partisan channels that had been implicitly incorporated as a nonproblematic part of the classic realignment model. People therefore looked for it with the wrong tools and in the wrong places."[4] Translation: for evidence of realignments, don't bother to rely on patterns of election returns any more. In the newer Burnham view, we need to look beyond "Type A" critical realignments, the trademark shakeups in voter alignments that inspired and defined the classical realignments genre and engrossed Key, Schattschneider, Sundquist, Burnham himself, and the rest to consider "Type B" critical realignments, which feature abrupt political changes of other kinds.[5] For support on this point, Burnham draws on two sources. One is "the very perceptive political commentator Sidney Blumenthal," with his idea of the "permanent campaign"—the decisive and lasting intrusion of campaign consultants into both elections and governing around 1968; Blumenthal "was perhaps the first to get the basic story right."[6]

---

4. Walter Dean Burnham, "Critical Realignment: Dead or Alive?" ch. 5 in Byron E. Shafer (ed.), *The End of Realignment? Interpreting American Electoral Eras* (Madison: University of Wisconsin Press, 1991), 107; italics in original.

5. Ibid., 116. At issue here is a distinction between two varieties of *abrupt* political change. This has nothing to do with the more familiar distinction between abrupt political change, as seen in classically defined electoral realignments, and gradual or secular electoral change.

6. Ibid., 107. The reference is to Sidney Blumenthal, *The Permanent Campaign* (New York: Simon and Schuster, rev. ed., 1982), 303–12.

The other source for Burnham is a study of the unquestionably turbulent 1960s and early 1970s by John H. Aldrich and Richard G. Niemi in which those years are de-
clared to be a "critical era" exhibiting "a wide variety
of changes" that inaugurated the country's "sixth party
system."[7] The old realignments calendar is accordingly
borne out. For this study, twenty-seven political indicators, none of which probes for an electoral realignment in
any conventional sense, were organized into time series
extending across four decades. In general, sharp changes
do indeed materialize in the indicators between 1964 and
1972. During that time, for example, confidence in government plummeted; positive attitudes toward the parties eroded; incumbency advantage in House elections
surged; African-American identification with the Democratic party solidified (in the mid-1960s); and the public's
designation of the country's "most important problem"
shifted from foreign to domestic concerns as the Vietnam
War wound down in the early 1970s. Also, on the structural side, the parties decisively switched away from conventions toward primaries as a means of nominating their

---

7. Burnham, "Critical Realignment: Dead or Alive?" 107; Walter Dean
Burnham, "Constitutional Moments and Punctuated Equilibria: A Political
Scientist Confronts Bruce Ackerman's *We the People*," *Yale Law Journal* 108
(1999), 2237–77, at 2258. The source is John H. Aldrich and Richard G.
Niemi, "The Sixth American Party System: Electoral Change, 1952–1992,"
ch. 5 in Stephen C. Craig (ed.), *Broken Contract? Changing Relationships Between Americans and Their Government* (Boulder, Colo.: Westview, 1996), 87.

presidential candidates.[8] That was the 1960s and early 1970s. Recently, Aldrich has speculated about the existence of a new "critical era" inaugurating a "seventh party system" thirty or so years later in the 1990s.[9]

In this work, I largely steer clear of questions about realignments happening or not happening since 1932. On the not-happening side, party decomposition and other accounts are at least plausible, and I leave it there. We should not ask too much of the realignments genre. A perspective that managed to illuminate the first century and a half of American political history, even if it has ceased to work in recent times for whatever reasons, would be an impressive achievement.

On the happening side, I am uneasy about Type B realignments. To give up on critical elections as a defining property is to sacrifice not only content—the flightless bird comes to mind—but also definitional constraint. In probing for Type B realignments, what are the rules for deciding what qualifies as a relevant indicator? Whatever the answer, the genre risks embarrassment with this move. It is vanishingly unlikely that the familiar periodization of the realignments genre—that is, 1800, 1828, 1860, 1896, and 1932—would survive a serious canvass of American

8. Aldrich and Niemi discuss this move in "The Sixth American Party System," 101–2, although it could not, or at least does not, figure among their twenty-seven indicators.

9. John H. Aldrich, "Political Parties in a Critical Era," *American Politics Quarterly* 27 (1999), 9–32, 10–11.

history for junctures of "party-system" change independent of critical elections. For one thing, unwelcome junctures would turn up. Consider the developments during
the Progressive era around 1912: a growing cohort of Socialist mayors; a switch to initiative, referendum, and recall procedures in the states; direct primaries in the states;
direct election of U.S. senators; a lurch, courtesy of Woodrow Wilson, toward what James W. Ceaser has called "individual candidate supremacy" in the selection of presidents;[10] a historic disempowering of party leadership in
the U.S. House (in 1910); and the appearance of a force-
ful Progressive faction among congressional Republicans
that lasted a quarter of a century into the New Deal years.
A party system marked by the impulses of the Progressive
era was emerging. Public opinion data, if the technology
could be transported backward to that time of ferment,
would probably add dozens more items.

Closer to the present, a decent case arises for 1948
through 1956 as a juncture rivaling 1964 through 1972.
That postwar decade saw the breakup of the "Solid South"
in presidential voting; civil rights and the Cold War as new
agenda items; a Red scare that crushed the once influential Communist or at least pro–Popular Front left in the
Democratic party, third parties, and labor unions; and actual patterns of durable voter realignment as impressive

10. James W. Ceaser, *Presidential Selection: Theory and Development*
(Princeton: Princeton University Press, 1979), 39.

as those for 1964–72 (more on this in Chapter 4).[11] Also, as presidential candidates awoke to television as an invaluable direct link to the public, the 1950s brought pioneering media techniques in Eisenhower's campaigns; the country's last multiballot nominating convention in 1952 (candidates could henceforth build nationwide coalitions on their own in advance of a convention); a surge in split party outcomes in congressional districts (one way for president, the other way for House) in 1956;[12] and an introduction to a new kind of normality as one party managed to win the presidency but not the House in 1956.[13] That was an arresting result for a presidential year as opposed to a midterm; it had been seen previously only in 1792, 1848, and 1876. Yet the pattern was to appear in seven of twelve presidential election years starting in 1956.[14] Divided party control of the government thus

11. In the present work, see table 4.1 and fig. 4.1. See also Jerome M. Clubb, William H. Flanigan, and Nancy H. Zingale, *Partisan Realignment: Voters, Parties, and Government in American History* (Beverly Hills, Calif.: Sage, 1980), 92–97, 105; Larry M. Bartels, "Electoral Continuity and Change, 1868–1996," *Electoral Studies* 17 (1998), 301–26, at 315. On the importance of the 1948 election, see J. Clark Archer and Peter J. Taylor, *Section and Party: A Political Geography of American Presidential Elections, from Andrew Jackson to Ronald Reagan* (New York: Wiley, 1981), 119, 135–36, 209.

12. Burnham, *Critical Elections and the Mainsprings*, 109.

13. For a similar discussion of the 1956 election as a break point, see Morris Fiorina, *Divided Government* (Boston: Allyn and Bacon, 2d ed., 1996), 12–13.

14. And very nearly in 1960, 1976, and 2000, albeit very nearly *not* in 1968.

came of age. In terms of party systems, construed broadly, much of the future seems to have been forged during 1948 through 1956.[15]

But that is enough. In the case of alleged Type B realignments, the rules are unclear and the past is uncharted. The subject of this book is electoral realignments, not nonelectoral realignments. My task is to appraise the familiar electoral realignments perspective—although without making too much of the absence of certifiable realignments after 1932, since that absence is perhaps excusable. Required is an examination of American electoral experience in general. The fifteen claims presented in Chapter 2 will be examined one by one and assessed for their empirical validity and, occasionally, their illuminative power.

15. Many of the developments I cite here for 1948–56 do not have much in common, yet that is no less true of those cited by Aldrich and Niemi for 1964–72.

The Cyclical Dynamic

4 DOES AMERICAN ELECTORAL HISTORY sort into specified crests and troughs? Do the highs and lows appear in regular cycles? What explains the regularity of the alleged cycles? Claims 1 through 4 of the realignments genre address these basic concerns.

1) *The existence of specified realigning and nonrealigning elections.* Of efforts to discover realigning as opposed to nonrealigning elections during American history, I am aware of two sophisticated works using quantitative data that were undertaken blind to the conventional wisdom of the realignments genre about what results to expect.[1] It

---

1. Peter F. Nardulli's recent work, which has interesting time series on subregions, does not seem to be "blind" in this sense. See Nardulli, "The Concept of a Critical Realignment, Electoral Behavior, and Political

should be said that no quantitative work on this subject can be unimpeachable. Countless decisions need to be made about data use. Coding of third parties is always a nightmare. Moreover, no one to my knowledge has tackled in any serious way the slippery and probably intractable task of detecting realigning eras as opposed to single critical elections. Still, impressive work has been done using data sets based on individual elections.

The work of Jerome M. Clubb, William H. Flanigan, and Nancy H. Zingale in 1980 is the first instance.[2] It uses an analysis of variance technique to examine presidential election returns for states (the states weighted statistically according to their total votes cast). Sensitive to the connotations of the realignments genre, Clubb, Flanigan, and Zingale probe for two distinct kinds of electoral change.[3]

Change," *American Political Science Review* 89 (1995), 10–22. On this aspect of Nardulli's work, see Larry M. Bartels, "Electoral Continuity and Change, 1868–1996," *Electoral Studies* 17 (1998), 301–26, at 324n15.

2. Jerome M. Clubb, William H. Flanigan, and Nancy H. Zingale, *Partisan Realignment: Voters, Parties, and Government in American History* (Beverly Hills, Calif.: Sage, 1980), ch. 3. This book is a model of clear exposition. For an earlier, somewhat different version of the work, see William H. Flanigan and Nancy H. Zingale, "The Measurement of Electoral Change," *Political Methodology* 1:3 (1974), 49–82. Results from the 1974 version are also reported in Walter Dean Burnham, Jerome H. Clubb, and William H. Flanigan, "Partisan Realignment: A Systemic Perspective," ch. 1 in Joel H. Silbey, Allan G. Bogue, and William H. Flanigan (eds.), *The History of American Electoral Behavior* (Princeton: Princeton University Press, 1978), 45–77, at 58–64.

3. The connotation of two possible kinds of realigning change, labeled

The first is "surge," as when, in a limiting case, every state swings 10 percent more Democratic in election year B as compared to previous election year A. This is a fitting accommodation of, for example, the Democrats' across-the-board sweep in 1932. The second kind is "interaction," as when, in a limiting case, half the states swing 10 percent more Democratic, the other half swing 10 percent more Republican, yet despite the considerable disruption in cleavage there is no (necessary) net national party percentage change between election years A and B. This might accommodate, for example, African-American voters shifting Democratic while southern white voters simultaneously shifted Republican in the 1960s. Often, elements of both kinds of change occur in the same election. For Clubb, Flanigan, and Zingale, either kind of change passes the test of being "realigning" if it persists during a span of succeeding elections—again, the necessary durability requirement of the realignments genre. Otherwise, any A-to-B change is merely "deviating."

Clubb, Flanigan, and Zingale proceed by analyzing successive election quadruplets (A through D, B through E, etc.)—the logic being to situate each individual election in a context of both its predecessors and its successors.

---

here as "surge" and "interaction," goes back to V. O. Key, Jr., "A Theory of Critical Elections," *Journal of Politics* 17 (1955), 3–18, at 11–13. It is embraced in Burnham, Clubb, and Flanigan, "Partisan Realignment," 50–53.

Their methodology requires them to calculate results separately for each party (because of third parties, one major
party's record is not just the mirror image of the other's).
This means that, in principle, any presidential election
can produce as many as four kinds of realigning change—
Democratic party surge, Democratic party interaction,
Republican party surge, and Republican party interaction. Surge change can take a plus or minus sign, whereas
interactive change does not take a sign. The analysis accommodates the Democrats beginning in 1836, the Republicans beginning in 1868. These were not the first elections that the two respective parties actually took part in,
but they were the first, given the before-and-after evidence
requirements of this technique, that could be statistically
accommodated.[4]

4. A similar consideration, and a problem, involves states: since the vote
of any state in any election needs to be compared with its votes in preceding
and succeeding elections, a state freshly admitted to the union cannot enter
into the analysis quickly. This causes trouble in the 1860s, when the Confed-
erate states seceded and were readmitted, and in the 1890s, when several
new states could not enter into the calculations for the 1896 election—even
though they cast presidential votes in 1896 and in most cases also previously
in 1892. Thus lost from the 1896 calculations are Idaho, Montana, North
Dakota, South Dakota, Utah, Washington, and Wyoming. This is unfortu-
nate for the analysis, since this was protest territory in the 1890s. These are
seven of the eleven states outside the South and border area carried by the
Populists in 1892 or Bryan in 1896. Still, it should be realized that these
seven states were lightly populated then. Altogether they cast 2.9 percent of
the national vote in 1896—less than did, for example, Kentucky, Iowa, Indiana or Missouri taken alone. The Populist strain has always looked bigger
on the map than it was in the actual vote. On the brighter side, for analytic
purposes, the four older nonsouthern-area states that voted for the Populists

For all presidential elections between 1836 and 1964, Clubb, Flanigan, and Zingale document the realignment changes of various kinds that they considered significant enough to report (see table 4.1).[5] The election of 1836, for example, produces a large realignment interaction value of 5.65 percent for the Democrats, who, in that year, without scoring any notable net gain or loss in votes, greatly rearranged the geography of their electoral base as the northerner Martin Van Buren succeeded the southerner Andrew Jackson as party nominee. To cite other examples, the Reconstruction era election of 1868 marks a realignment surge of 6.09 percent for the Democrats, the Truman-Dewey election of 1948 a negative "realignment surge" (that is, a loss) of 8.20 percent for the Democrats, and the post–World War I Harding-Cox election of 1920 a realignment surge of 7.73 percent for the Republicans. Again, all the values in table 4.1 are calculated to reflect long-lasting, not just deviating, electoral change.

How do the specified dates of the realignments calendar fare in table 4.1? The election of 1932 performs spectacularly in these calculations: That year's realignment surges of 16.28 percent for the Democrats and −11.33 percent for the Republicans are the best and worst ever

---

in 1892 or Bryan in 1896—Colorado, Kansas, Nebraska, and Nevada—cast 5.4 percent of the national vote in 1896 and are accommodated in the analysis. On the problem of the noncountable new states of the 1890s, see Clubb, Flanigan, and Zingale, *Partisan Realignment*, 89, 100.

5. Ibid., table 3.1a, at 92–93.

Table 4.1. Surge and Interactive Realignment in Presidential Elections, 1836–1964, as Calculated by Clubb, Flanigan, and Zingale

	Presidential Candidates		Democratic Vote		Republican Vote*	
Year	Democrat	Republican (or Whig)	Surge	Inter-action	Surge	Inter-action
1836	Van Buren	(3 Whigs)		5.65	—	—
1840	Van Buren	Harrison	−3.61		—	—
1844	Polk	Clay			—	—
1848	Cass	Taylor	−5.59		—	—
1852	Pierce	Scott			—	—
1856	Buchanan	Fremont			—	—
1860	Douglas	Lincoln		2.80	—	—
1864	McClellan	Lincoln		1.65		
1868	Seymour	Grant	+6.09			
1872	Greeley	Grant				
1876	Tilden	Hayes	+1.45		−4.68	
1880	Hancock	Garfield				
1884	Cleveland	Blaine				
1888	Cleveland	Harrison				
1892	Cleveland	Harrison				
1896	Bryan	McKinley			+5.16	
1900	Bryan	McKinley				
1904	Parker	Roosevelt		1.14		
1908	Bryan	Taft				
1912	Wilson	Taft				
1916	Wilson	Hughes				
1920	Cox	Harding	−1.77		+7.73	
1924	Davis	Coolidge				
1928	Smith	Hoover		1.92		

Table 4.1. *Continued*

| Year | Presidential Candidates | | Democratic Vote | | Republican Vote* | |
	Democrat	Republican (or Whig)	Surge	Inter-action	Surge	Inter-action
1932	Roosevelt	Hoover	+16.28		−11.33	
1936	Roosevelt	Landon				1.20
1940	Roosevelt	Willkie				
1944	Roosevelt	Dewey				
1948	Truman	Dewey	−8.20	1.15		
1952	Stevenson	Eisenhower			+2.47	1.26
1956	Stevenson	Eisenhower				
1960	Kennedy	Nixon	+1.30			
1964	Johnson	Goldwater		2.06	−2.45	1.16

Source: Clubb, Flanigan, and Zingale, *Partisan Realignment*, table 3.1a, 92–93.
*Values for the Republican party cannot be calculated before 1868.

experienced by either party. The election of 1860 is something of a washout, but that may be understandable. No comparative statistical analysis can easily accommodate the Democratic party's breakup into competing northern and southern factions during the election of that crisis year. (Yet note that the Republicans' fragmentation into competing Taft and Theodore Roosevelt factions in the 1912 election poses the same problem.) But how about the election of 1896? That election does register in table 4.1— the Republicans enjoyed a sizable realignment surge of 5.16 percent—yet on balance the 1896 election does not outperform those of 1836, 1848, 1868, 1876, 1920, 1948, or 1964, to say nothing of 1932.[6]

The second researcher probing for critical elections is Larry M. Bartels, in 1998.[7] Although using a different statistical technique, he also relies on aggregate state-level election data, weights the states according to their total votes cast, considers each presidential election in the context of its predecessors and successors, and is sensitive to both surge and interactive varieties of change (though those are not his terms) if they prove to be durable.[8] The realigning aftereffects of each election are traced for a quarter of a century. The basic indicator for the years 1868 through 1996—which rules out any reading for 1860—is

6. For 1876, 1920, 1932, 1948, and 1964, the appearance of entries in more than one column of the table needs to be considered somehow. Using the same methodology as that underpinning table 4.1 of this vol., Clubb, Flanigan, and Zingale also report national realignment results for the U.S. House vote, aggregated by state, for elections between 1838 and 1966. Midterms as well as presidential-year elections are included. Briefly, significant realigning change does occur in the congressional vote in the mid-1890s—it is chiefly associated with the Republican midterm sweep of 1894. Considerably more impressive, however, is the realigning change associated with the post–Mexican War (and Wilmot Proviso) election of 1848, the late Reconstruction midterm of 1874, the anti-Republican-establishment midterm of 1910, the post–World War I election of 1920, and of course the Depression election of 1932. Rivaling the mid-1890s is the first Eisenhower midterm of 1954—a surge year for the Democrats that initiated forty years of House supremacy. The House elections around 1860 do not make much of a showing (ibid., 94–97).

7. Bartels, "Electoral Continuity and Change," 313–17.

8. Bartels also encounters the problem of the noncountable, newly admitted states in the Reconstruction era and the 1890s (ibid., 324n9).

the Republican minus the Democratic percentage of the popular vote for president by state. The calculations end in one distilled national realignment score for each election. In Bartels's summary graph, the election of 1932 emerges as the runaway winner in "average effect, 25-year horizon," which is the distilled score (see figure 4.1).[9] As in Clubb, Flanigan, and Zingale, the realigning consequences of 1932 are in a class by themselves. But after that, what? An easy second-place finisher is the post-Reconstruction election featuring Garfield against Hancock in 1880, followed by, in descending order, the Harding-Cox election of 1920, the Nixon-McGovern election of 1972, Franklin Roosevelt's second election in 1936, the Hayes-Tilden election of 1876, Wilson's initial election in the multiparty contest of 1912, the McKinley-Bryan election of 1896, and Coolidge's reelection in the three-party contest of 1924.

From the standpoint of the realignments genre, leaving aside the anomalous election of 1860, with its fragmented Democrats, there is a problem here. Given only these Clubb, Flanigan, and Zingale and Bartels analyses, probably not one reader in a hundred would seize on the elections of 1896 and 1932 as a distinct pair of post-1860s realigning events. The 1896 election does not perform well

9. Ibid., 315, fig. 8.

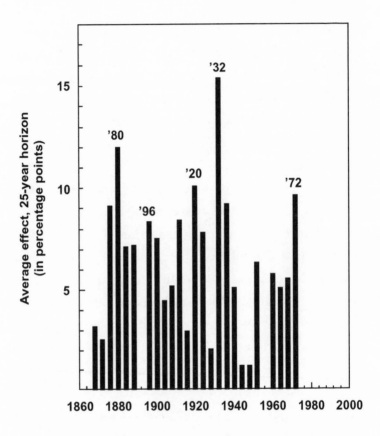

Fig. 4.1. Critical Elections, 1868–1972

Source: Reprinted from *Electoral Studies*, vol. 17, Larry M. Bartels,
"Electoral Continuity and Change, 1868–1896," p. 315, 1998, with
permission from Elsevier Service.

enough for that.[10] Let it be repeated that short-term, deviating electoral change is one thing; long-term, realigning change is another. There is little doubt that the 1896 election stands out for its short-term change.[11] Indeed, 1896 can be made to generate one of three tall spikes on a graph along with 1860 and 1932 if the calculation is simply of "first differences"—that is, the differences in voting patterns between any given elections and their immediate predecessors, in the present case 1896 versus 1892.[12] But that is not realigning change. In Bartels's assessment: "The electoral pattern established in 1896 was much less durable than previous scholarship has suggested. . . . The electoral impetus of 1896 was diminished by half within four years; the state-by-state voting pattern in 1900 reflected the divisions of 1888 . . . as much or more than those of

10. On this point, see also Allan J. Lichtman, "Political Realignment and 'Ethnocultural' Voting in Late Nineteenth Century America," *Journal of Social History* 16 (1982–83), 55–82, at 59–61.

11. See Clubb, Flanigan, and Zingale, *Partisan Realignment*, 98, 100, 101; Bartels, "Electoral Continuity and Change," 312, 316; J. Clark Archer and Peter J. Taylor, *Section and Party: A Political Geography of American Presidential Elections, from Andrew Jackson to Ronald Reagan* (New York: Wiley, 1981), 79, 119, 129–34, 208–9.

12. Such a chart appears for the Democratic party vote in Burnham, Clubb, and Flanigan, "Partisan Realignment," 51. Helping along the 1892-to-1896 spike in this chart, however, is a scoring of the 1892 Democratic vote at zero in several states where the Democratic parties had strategically "fused" with Populists behind the Populist presidential candidate (ibid., 62). On the fusion deals, see Walter Dean Burnham, *Presidential Ballots, 1836–1892* (Baltimore: Johns Hopkins University Press, 1955), 149, 153, 931, 953.

1896."[13] The much noticed 1896 result comes to look suspiciously like a "deviating" one.

In the face of numbers and reflections like these, how can the 1896 election be kept on its canonical pedestal? That would seem to be an early assignment for any backer of the realignments genre. One not entirely implausible move is to argue that all such quantitative analysis is impeachable and that at any rate, quantitative analysis by itself cannot bring out the full meaning and content of coalitional reconfigurations. Needed also is relevant contextual information about such matters as intensities of viewpoint, signal events, accompanying pyrotechnics, and dramatic development. Certainly the decade of the 1890s offers a rich supply of such material. There was the Populist revolt in 1892, the second worst depression of American history beginning in 1893,[14] the astounding, still unmatched 120-seat shift to the Republicans in the House midterm elections of 1894,[15] the fracturing of both major parties over silver prices and other questions in the nominating processes of 1896, the capture of the Democratic party by anti–Wall Street insurgents led by Bryan in 1896, Bryan's transfixing "Cross of Gold" speech, Bryan's unprecedented speechmaking campaign across the coun-

13. Bartels, "Electoral Continuity and Change," 316.

14. On that depression, see Charles Hoffmann, "The Depression of the Nineties," *Journal of Economic History* 16 (1956), 137–64; Paul W. Glad, *McKinley, Bryan, and the People* (Philadelphia: Lippincott, 1964), ch. 4.

15. See Glad, *McKinley, Bryan, and the People,* 91–94.

try,[16] Mark Hanna's landmark mobilization of corporate money and influence behind McKinley, and the era of Republican dominance that resulted. It is a familiar and riveting story.

But other such stories exist, even if, partly courtesy of the realignments genre, they may not be quite as prominent in the political science lore. In light of the good showing of the 1876 election in both the Clubb, Flanigan, and Zingale and Bartels calculations, as well as the 1880 election in Bartels's, and in line with the realignment genre's practice of weaving narratives about short sequences of arguably related elections (that is, not just one election), consider the following stylized account I wrote for this occasion:[17]

> In the 1874 congressional midterm, spurred by Reconstruction fatigue and a weak economy, the American electorate produced one of its most decisive results ever—a sweeping Democratic takeover of the House that rendered federal Reconstruction policy unsustainable. The state Republican regime in Mississippi soon crumbled, paving the way for the extraordinary election campaign waged by white "Redeemers" to take back South Carolina in 1876—a successful politico-military drive conducted largely by army veterans that featured

16. See, e.g., John Gerring, *Party Ideologies in America, 1828–1996* (New York: Cambridge University Press, 1998), 190–91.

17. On this subject, see also Michael W. McConnell, "The Forgotten Constitutional Moment," *Constitutional Commentary* 11 (1994), 115–44, at 122–40. For a response to this piece, see Bruce Ackerman, *We the People: Transformations* (Cambridge: Harvard University Press, 1998), 471–74.

guerrilla organization, intimidation, and murder.[18] This innovative mix would be seen again in Germany and Italy after World War I. At the national level, the tense presidential contest of 1876 ended in a hung result and, for the only time in American history, an extraconstitutional settlement. Involving an ad hoc commission, this was a cross-party, cross-regional deal that has been brought to life in possibly the most distinguished work ever written about the events surrounding an American election—C. Vann Woodward's *Reunion and Reaction.*[19] In effect, the Republicans kept control of the presidency, but southern Democratic whites gained control of their home affairs: In the South, it was to be whites on top, blacks down, and Yankees out. Full African-American disfranchisement came a generation later, but that was an aftereffect. The question of dominance was settled. Redeemer governments came to enjoy solid control of the South by the late 1870s—notably of South Carolina (historically the Deep South's style-setter in political matters), Mississippi, and Louisiana, the chief spots of contention by virtue of their having African-American population majorities, or approximately that. To put it one way, democracy at the national level having been tried and failed, the United States reverted to its pre-1860 standing as what might be called a consociational republic—a pragmatic arrangement, now minus slavery of course, between North and South.

In its southern aspect, the 1876–77 settlement was so

18. Richard Zuczek, "The Last Campaign of the Civil War: South Carolina and the Revolution of 1876," *Civil War History* 42 (1996), 18–31; Zuczek, *State of Rebellion: Reconstruction in South Carolina* (Columbia: University of South Carolina Press, 1996), chs. 8, 9.

19. C. Vann Woodward, *Reunion and Reaction: The Compromise of 1877 and the End of Reconstruction* (Boston: Little, Brown, 1951).

unusual that it has seldom figured in cross-national analysis—it entailed constitutional politics for one race, but a caste system and suppression for another. The nearest analogy may be the South African Nationalist election victory of 1948. In terms of voting statistics, the full effect of the 1876–77 settlement was not felt until 1880, when notably Louisiana and South Carolina, which had narrowly voted Republican at the presidential level in 1876—the beleaguered biracial Republicans still controlled the ballot count then at that office level[20]— swung dramatically to the Democratic column where they stayed for generations. After that, no deep-southern state voted Republican again in a presidential election until 1956. In major respects, the southern electoral victories of the mid-1870s determined (to use Schatt- schneider's verb, which works better here than in most contexts owing to the not easily reversible suppression of southern African-Americans) the course of American politics and society for the bulk of a century until the civil rights revolution of the 1960s unraveled them.

Not the least of the aftermaths of the 1876–77 settle- ment was an abrupt shift in the national policy agenda. Slavery, war, and Reconstruction issues that had con- vulsed the country for a generation receded. Civil rights was largely abandoned—not least by a Supreme Court that could read the election returns of the 1870s.[21] Presi- dents took to modernizing the executive branch through civil service reform, wrestling with the tariff, and impos- ing order in industrial relations—as did the Republican

20. For a recent treatment, see Ronald F. King, "Hayes Truly Won: A Revisionist Analysis of the 1876 Electoral Vote in Louisiana, South Carolina and Florida," paper presented at the annual conference of the American Political Science Association, Washington, D.C., September 2000.

21. See McConnell, "The Forgotten Constitutional Moment," 133–40.

Hayes by deploying federal troops in the national rail-
way strike of 1877 and, later, the Democrat Cleveland in
the Pullman strike of 1894.

This contextual sketch is meant to be exemplary, not
exhaustive, of ones that might compete with a sketch of
the 1890s. The 1870s story holds up well against that of the
1890s, and, as reported earlier, the statistics generated by
Clubb, Flanigan, and Zingale and Bartels for 1876 and
1880 at least match those for 1896. In a separate analysis
of the congressional vote by Clubb, Flanigan, and Zingale,
also probing for realigning change, the 1874 midterm easily dominates that of 1894 and is surpassed only by the on-
year House election of 1932 and possibly the midterm of
1910.[22] Burnham himself, in an early probe for "discontinuity" in presidential voting, came up with uniquely, indeed "spectacularly" high readings for the year 1874 (in its
role not as midterm but as the statistical midpoint in a
sequence of ten presidential elections, as compared with
the midpoints of twenty-six other such sequences of ten
elections).[23] It seems a good bet that if the 1876 election
had taken place thirty years after 1860 rather than when it
did, we would have heard about it quite a while ago as a
realigning election.

To recapitulate, neither statistics nor stories bear out

22. Clubb, Flanigan, and Zingale, *Partisan Realignment*, 94–97.
23. Walter Dean Burnham, *Critical Elections and the Mainsprings of
American Politics* (New York: Norton, 1970), 13–17, at 13, 15.

the canonical realignments calendar of 1860, 1896, and 1932. Something like faith seems to be needed to keep it in place. In particular, to cite the instances discussed here, there is no reason whatever to elevate the 1890s over the 1870s as a realigning juncture. Occasionally in the realignments genre, the mid-1870s is embraced as a lesser, "mid-sequence" juncture of electoral change tucked halfway between the larger events of the 1860s and 1890s. But that is a dodge. On the evidence, no such privileging of the 1890s over the 1870s is warranted.

To close with a more general point, note that the evidence in table 4.1 and figure 4.1 does not favor the basic idea of sorting elections into two distinct types any more than it does the particular highlighted junctures of the realignments calendar (1932 aside). Dichotomization does not pan out. Bartels casts doubt on it: "Rather than consisting of a few great peaks separated by broad plateaus reflecting long periods of political stasis, the distribution of long-term effects in [Figure 2.1] reflects a complex intermixture of large, medium, and small effects."[24] Clubb, Flanigan, and Zingale cast doubt on any model of crests and troughs: "Far more indications of realigning change appear than can seemingly be tolerated by any simple view of American electoral history as

24. Bartels, "Electoral Continuity and Change," 315.

characterized by prolonged periods of stability punctuated by occasional electoral upheavals."[25]

2) *Periodicity*. This discussion can be brief. If the identities of realigning elections are in question, then their periodicity is in question. Above all, it is crucial not to let periodicity dictate identity. In this regard, it would be well to take a close look at the election of 1828, which brought Andrew Jackson to power. Important as that contest was, exactly what justifies its reputation as distinctively a realigning election? I have not seen a serious defense of the idea. "The election of 1828 was not fought over great issues," Glyndon G. Van Deusen has written. "Questions important to the nation, it is true, were before the public eye—the tariff, land policy, internal improvements—but on these questions there were no clear-cut party stands."[26] There is little support for the distinctiveness of 1828 in Richard P. McCormick's pioneering 1967 essay on the so-called "second American party system," where the elections of 1824, 1836, and 1840 all rival that of 1828 as gateways to a new party era.[27] If a single break-point date

25. Clubb, Flanigan, and Zingale, *Partisan Realignment*, 105; see also 115.

26. Glyndon G. Van Deusen, *The Jacksonian Era, 1828–1848* (New York: Harper and Row, 1959), 27.

27. Richard P. McCormick, "Political Development and the Second Party System," ch. 4 in William N. Chambers and Walter Dean Burnham (eds.), *The American Party Systems: Stages of Political Development* (New

needs to be chosen as the beginning of a new era, William G. Shade suggests 1836;[28] Joel H. Silbey argues for 1838.[29] In statistical terms, using states as units, there is virtually no relation between the voter cleavage of 1836, when Van Buren ran for president, and the three previous elections when Jackson ran (losing once and winning twice).[30] The problem with break points in the late 1830s, of course, from the standpoint of the realignments calendar, is that they ruin its alleged periodicity. They usher in a "party system" that is all too brief.[31] The new Whig-Democratic competition collapsed in the mid-1850s.

York: Oxford University Press, 1967), 91–102. See also Richard P. McCormick, *The Second American Party System: Party Formation in the Jacksonian Era* (Chapel Hill: University of North Carolina Press, 1966), ch. 7.

28. William G. Shade, "Political Pluralism and Party Development: The Creation of a Modern Party System: 1815–1852," ch. 3 in Paul Kleppner (ed.), *The Evolution of American Electoral Systems* (Westport, Conn.: Greenwood, 1981), 82, 83, 91, 103–4. See also Archer and Taylor, *Section and Party*, 79, 82–84, 207.

29. Joel H. Silbey, "Beyond Realignment and Realignment Theory: American Political Eras, 1789–1989," ch. 1 in Byron E. Shafer (ed.), *The End of Realignment?: Interpreting American Electoral Eras* (Madison: University of Wisconsin Press, 1991), 8–13.

30. Shade, "Political Pluralism and Party Development," 82, 83; Clubb, Flanigan, and Zingale, *Partisan Realignment*, 92; Gerald Pomper, "Classification of Presidential Elections," ch. 1 in Joel H. Silbey and Samuel T. McSeveney (eds.), *Voters, Parties, and Elections: Quantitative Essays in the History of American Popular Voting Behavior* (Lexington, Mass.: Xerox College Publishing, 1972), 8–17.

31. Richard P. McCormick points to "the relatively brief duration of this [second] party system." In his assessment, the system lasted only from 1840 through 1852. See *The Second American Party System*, 14, 341, 353, at 353.

How about the two hypothesized causes of realignment cycles?

3) *Cyclical Motor 1: Stress, tensions, flash points, boiling points.* A long buildup of stress ending in explosion is a familiar idea and, sometimes at any rate, a plausible model of reality. One thinks of, for example, the growing intensity of discontent among African-Americans between the mid-1950s and the mid-1960s or the anti–Vietnam War cause that accelerated between the mid-1960s and the early 1970s. Good instances can be found on the realignments calendar: the growing tension between the North and the South between 1854 and 1860 (though that had evidently also happened between 1844 and 1850 without triggering a realignment or a civil war) and possibly the growing discontent among farmers (though the pattern seems not to have been monotonic), particularly in the dryer plains states west of Missouri and Iowa during the decade and a half or so, ending in the Populist movement around 1890.

But a general theory of periodic, long-term stress buildups? That seems dubious. For one thing, if the canonical realignment junctures are respected, it would have to be shown that politically relevant stress, somehow indexed or at least convincingly argued for, was abnormally high in 1892 and 1928. Those were the years just before the onsets of the devastating and unquestionably stress-inducing depressions of 1893 and 1929. Possibly that could be shown for 1892 (even east of the plains and out-side the Cotton Belt), although we would need to see and appraise the argument; it has to be realized that in any society at any time there exists at least some level of stress or tension of one kind or another. But it is a near certainty that no such stress case could be made for 1928, when an electorate enjoying record-shattering prosperity made it virtually impossible for Al Smith to gain issue traction. In effect, he had to wage an uphill struggle against burgeoning stock prices, consumer durables, and movie and radio entertainment. We have good reason to believe that, absent the abrupt economic downturn in 1929, voters would have kept on electing presidents like Coolidge and Hoover for quite a while.[32]

At least one serious error lurks in the realignments genre's model of stress buildup: a tendency to elongate political troubles backward in time without warrant. To account for the Republican successes in 1894 and 1896,

---

32. Has Al Gore's loss in 2000 undermined this idea about the political benefits of prosperity? Probably not. It seems that the election of 2000 was not even an outlier in the familiar time-series analysis of presidential elections using economic and other explanatory variables—*if* annual growth rate in real disposable income per capita is substituted for annual growth rate in Gross Domestic Product (GDP) per capita as the key economic variable. According to the disposable-income standard, the record of the U.S. economy was not all that impressive in calendar 2000. Money was piling up in the government surplus, not in voters' pockets. See Larry M. Bartels and John Zaller, "Presidential Vote Models: A Recount," *PS: Political Science and Politics* 34 (March 2001), 9–20. Of course, one outlier is not likely to invalidate a statistical generalization anyway.

the 1893 depression is probably sufficient (although the apparently deviating shape of the 1896 result would no doubt have been different without a Bryan insurgency). To account for the Democratic successes in 1930 and 1932, the Depression that started in 1929 is enough. Both the 1890s and the 1930s can probably get along without long-term stress buildup as a causal ingredient. On the latter case, Sundquist agrees: "As late as the summer of 1929, there was little evidence of strain in the party system that had been established more than thirty years before." Then a "sudden cataclysmic event" intruded.[33]

4) *Cyclical Motor 2: Decay of party identification*. For this alternative explanation to work, it needs to be true that party identification has distinctively ebbed during the periods twenty-five years or so after the alleged past electoral realignments—notably during the 1850s, the 1880s and early 1890s, the 1920s, and the 1960s. Has that in fact happened? The answer is yes for the 1960s, although it is not clear what that proves, given the structural trend then toward candidate-centered politics. For previous times, a good deal of ingenuity has gone into addressing the ebb question indirectly, since direct evidence on party identification is lacking. Two inquiries have angled after the alleged 1920s ebb by drawing on opinion surveys of voters

33. James L. Sundquist, *Dynamics of the Party System: Alignment and Realignment of Political Parties in the United States* (Washington, D.C.: Brookings Institution, 1983), 48, 299; see also 198, 313.

of various age cohorts conducted after 1950. Is it true, so far as can be told from "recall" data in surveys, that voters coming of age *before* the New Deal era picked up their parents' party identifications less successfully than did voters coming of age *just after* the New Deal? (The latter time of especially well-cemented parental loyalties is the span when, according to theory, socialization should have worked best.)[34] Also, in post-1950 surveys, did the 1920s generation exhibit weaker party identifications than, as theory might predict, the New Deal generation?[35] To both of these questions, the answer is resoundingly no. The converse is true; better parental transmission and stronger identifications are the story for the 1920s generation, not for the relevant later cohorts. This result points to gentle party decline across many decades (or simply to stronger identifications through aging in the case of the latter indicator)—not to a valley-peak-valley realignment model.

Other probes have followed the logic: "If party identification in fact ebbed at designated past times—again, the

34. See the data in Clubb, Flanigan, and Zingale, *Partisan Realignment*, 124–27. On the expectation, see Paul Allen Beck, "A Socialization Theory of Partisan Realignment," ch. 10 in Richard G. Niemi and associates, *The Politics of Future Citizens* (San Francisco: Jossey-Bass, 1974), 206–7.

35. Jerome M. Clubb, William H. Flanigan, and Nancy H. Zingale, "Realignment and Political Generations," in *Research in Micropolitics* 1 (1986), 35–63, at 49–54. For relevant data, see also Warren E. Miller and J. Merrill Shanks, *The New American Voter* (Cambridge: Harvard University Press, 1996), 156.

1850s, the 1880s and early 1890s, the 1920s, the 1960s— then as a consequence some specified derivative X must have occurred at distinctively those times: Did X occur at distinctively those times?" Several Xs have been posited and pursued. (One, third-party movements, I take up in Chapter 5.) In party terms, for example, has voting for governor or (beginning in 1916) senator distinctively deviated from voting for president during the alleged past ebb times? According to aggregate state-level election data from 1876 through 1984, the answer is certainly no for governor and at best unclear for senator.[36] Has House voting distinctively deviated from presidential voting at the alleged past ebb times? In excellent graphs prepared by Clubb, Flanigan, and Zingale for, separately, the Democratic vote from 1824 through 1976 and the Republican vote from 1856 through 1976, I do not see any such pattern. Generally speaking, for example, the 1860s and 1870s exhibit more deviation than the 1880s; the 1910s as much as the 1920s; the 1950s as much as the 1960s. Again citing calculations by Clubb, Flanigan, and Zingale (which I will not explain here), is it true that "deviating" electoral change, or the impact of "short-term forces," or deviation from "normal voting patterns established early in [a] realignment era" has distinctly peaked during the

36. Walter Dean Burnham, "Periodization Schemes and 'Party Systems': The 'System of 1896' as a Case in Point," *Social Science History* 10 (1986), 263–313, at 293–96. Included are nonsouthern states only.

alleged past ebb times? The results are not very accommodating. The 1880s flunks expectations entirely on the first two measures, the 1920s is disappointing on the third, and the volatile election of 1912—an off-schedule event in the argument at hand—intrudes embarrassingly in all three cases.[37] Two other data exercises that are relevant, although they were not undertaken with the realignments calendar in mind, are Bartels's measures of "strengths of party loyalties" and "electoral volatility" for all presidential elections from 1868 through 1996. Before World War II, the elections notably free of past party loyalties were those of, in descending order of magnitude, 1928, 1932, 1872, 1912, 1936, 1884, and 1876; notably volatile were those of 1932, 1920, and 1912. The decade of the 1920s performs decently enough here—although other interpretations of the 1920 and 1928 elections are certainly possible—but virtually nothing in these Bartels calculations helps along the 1880s and early 1890s as a distinct ebb period, or for that matter the election of 1896 as a realignment.[38]

For all the diligence and inventiveness shown in these measures, the effect, Bartels aside, is of trying to hang items on a nonexistent rack. In this vein, recall Beck's

37. Clubb, Flanigan, and Zingale, *Partisan Realignment*, House voting at 144–47; deviating change at 140–43; short-term forces at 138–40; deviation from early patterns at 148–49.

38. Bartels, "Electoral Continuity and Change," strengths of loyalties at 306–9, fig. 2 at 308; volatility at 320–23, fig. 10 at 321.

reasoning that although societal traumas like those of the 1860s, 1890s, and 1930s could trigger realignments, "other traumas of at least equal magnitude—the economic depressions of 1873 and 1907, two world wars, and the anticommunist hysteria of the early cold war period, for example—had no more than short-lived impacts on partisan behavior."[39] But some of those other traumas *did* have long-lived impacts on partisan behavior: going by the measures of "realigning" change by Clubb, Flanigan, and Zingale and Bartels, the cases for the depression of 1873 and World War I are at least as good as that for the depression of 1893. On the evidence, the canonical realignments calendar is not a secure enough baseline to reason or plot research from.

In short, party identification does not seem to succeed any better as a cyclical motor than do tension and boiling points. This is not to deny that traumatic events can lastingly affect party identification. V. O. Key wrote in 1952: "So cohesive were the bonds of party [after the Civil War] that for sixty years the country was 'normally' Republican. . . . It remained for a second catastrophe, the Great Depression, to produce a major alternation in the pattern of partisan division within the voting population."[40] War-

---

39. Beck, "A Socialization Theory of Partisan Realignment," 212.
40. V. O. Key, Jr., "The Future of the Democratic Party," *Virginia Quarterly Review* 28 (1952), 161–75, at 163. The intervening sentence in this quotation is: "Even in the crucial election of 1896, the Republican coalition

ren E. Miller and J. Merrill Shanks were still making that case in 1996: "During the first two periods [that is, those of the Civil War and the Great Depression], the perspectives of each age, once established, shaped the partisanship of families and communities for generations to come."[41] Note, however, that this old commonsensical idea says nothing about the 1820s, the 1890s, periodicity, or thirty-year cycles.

That is my case regarding dichotomized election types, periodicity, and dynamics. None of the claims of the re-alignments genre holds up well.

---

fought off the threat of the Western silver and agrarian radicals and by the promise of the full dinner pail held the support of most industrial workers."

41. Miller and Shanks, *The New American Voter,* 132; see also 184.

Processes and Issues

5 DISAPPOINTING RESULTS LIKE THOSE reported above, however, do not end the discussion. Realignments advocates are quick with arguments of the form: "Even if patterns A, B, C, and D don't pan out, patterns E, F, G, and H will." Hence the advisability of assessing many alleged patterns.

In this chapter I take up three claims of the realignments genre bearing on processes and three bearing on issues. My strategy in each of the six cases is to investigate how well the relevant kinds of events or features of American history have mapped onto the realignments calendar—that is, the calendar of 1828, 1860, 1896, and 1932. In all six cases, some specified mapping has been theorized.

5) *Voter concern and turnout.* Has voter concern or turnout peaked at the accepted realignment junctures? "Concern," though in principle distinct from turnout, may be intractable. Voter turnout is measurable. For any election, the long-standing custom is to calculate the number of voters as numerator over the number of those eligible to vote as denominator. I follow that convention here, although note that the resulting time series masks the abrupt changes in the denominator brought about by the Fifteenth Amendment, which enfranchised African-Americans in 1870, and the Nineteenth Amendment which enfranchised women in 1920. These changes in denominator, which were deposits of, respectively, the Reconstruction era and some combination of the Progressive era and World War I, have certainly been two of the leading hinge points in American history regarding voter participation.

But to stick with the conventional ratio definition, has voter turnout measured in this way peaked as hypothesized? Statistics for relevant eras reflect upturns, downturns, and periods of relative stability (see fig. 5.1).[1] The nineteenth-century record is at least not hostile to the idea. In the long span of sixteen high-participation elections from 1840 through 1900, when turnout dipped only

1. Source: United States Bureau of the Census, *Historical Statistics of the United States, Colonial Times to 1970* (Washington, D.C.: U.S. Government Printing Office, 1975), vol. 2, 1067–72.

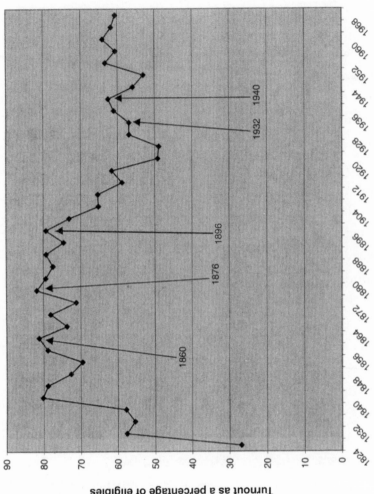

Fig. 5.1. Voter Turnout in Presidential Elections

once below 70 percent (that was in 1852), the highest val-
ues are for 1876 (81.8 percent), 1860 (81.2 percent), the
Harrison–Van Buren election of 1840 (80.2 percent), the
Garfield-Hancock election of 1880 (79.4 percent), the
Harrison-Cleveland election of 1888 (79.3 percent), and
the McKinley-Bryan election of 1896 (also 79.3 percent).
The 1860 and 1896 elections score well here, although
note that the highest turnout during this span, and in fact
during all of American history, is that of 1876. The end of
Reconstruction strikes again.[2]

How about the twentieth century?[3] As it happens, no
one examining the relevant time series would pick out
1932 as a high-turnout election. It is not even a close
call. In the vicinity of 1932, what catches the eye is a nearly
monotonic, rather steep rise in turnout between 1920 and
1940. In percentage of eligibles voting, 1940 surpassed
1932 by 62.5 percent to 56.9 percent. The 1940 peak is
thought provoking: Was it the imminence of war that
brought voters out? Later peaks during the twentieth
century are those of Eisenhower's first election in 1952
(63.3 percent) and the Kennedy-Nixon election of 1960
(64.0 percent).[4] On balance across the two centuries of

2. On the 1876 peak, see also John R. Petrocik, *Party Coalitions: Realignments and the Decline of the New Deal Party System* (Chicago: University of
Chicago Press, 1981), 35, 157.

3. See the section on the "System of 1896" in Chapter 6 of this volume
for a discussion of the turnout slump of the early twentieth century.

4. U.S. Bureau of the Census, *Historical Statistics*, vol. 2, 1067–72. As

American history, the fit between high turnout and alleged realignments is modest at best; no one informed of just the turnout statistics would come anywhere near guessing the realignments.

6) *Turmoil in presidential nominating conventions.* At issue here is whether nominating conventions tend to lapse from their "usual integrative functions" during re-alignment junctures and instead "themselves contribute to polarization."[5] This calls for a coding of conventions according to their "integrative success," yet I have not come across any indicator that does that task convinc-ingly. Beck, for a measure of convention "harmony," uses the number of ballots required to select a party's presi-dential nominee.[6] In general, however, that measure is a doubtful guide to integrative success. The Republican convention of 1880 took thirty-six ballots to nominate Garfield, and the Democratic convention of 1912 took forty-six ballots to nominate Wilson, but those parties did not suffer serious integrative problems in those years. In reality, a multiple-ballot convention may be no more dis-abling to a party than a multiple-candidate primary. On

is well known, the time-series curve slopes gradually downward after the 1960s.

5. Walter Dean Burnham, *Critical Elections and the Mainsprings of American Politics* (New York: Norton, 1970), 7.

6. Paul Allen Beck, "The Electoral Cycle and Patterns of American Poli-tics," *British Journal of Political Science* 9 (1979), 129–56, at 142.

the other hand, the Republicans took only one ballot to nominate Taft in 1912, and the Democrats only one to nominate Humphrey in 1968, yet both those conventions set new standards in intraparty polarization.[7]

I shall resort to common sense and, I hope, relevant facts. Here is a list of conventions at which a significant segment of a party departed a convention refusing to support its party's just-chosen presidential nominee or at which—this is an escape clause—something else happened that was spectacularly polarizing.

- In 1844, the Van Buren faction of the Democratic party rejected a vice-presidential nomination designed to appease them.
- In 1848, the New York Barnburner faction (the Van Burenites) refused an offer to be seated at the Democratic convention.
- In 1860, the Democrats famously broke up into northern and southern factions that waged their separate presidential campaigns.
- In 1896, twenty-four silver delegates from the western states walked out of the Republican convention.
- Also in 1896, 162 gold delegates, violating the custom of unanimous consent after a winner goes over

7. For data on convention ballots through 1956, see Paul T. David, Ralph M. Goldman, and Richard C. Bain, *The Politics of National Party Conventions* (Washington, D.C.: Brookings Institution, 1960), 428–31.

the top, refused to vote for Bryan at the Democratic convention.[8]

- In 1912, 348 Theodore Roosevelt delegates, ready to bolt to the Progressive cause, refused to vote for Taft at the Republican convention.

- In 1924, the two leading factions at the Democratic convention clashed over whether to denounce the Ku Klux Klan and deadlocked for two weeks over a presidential nominee, taking a record 103 ballots to nominate John W. Davis. (This is one instance where multiple balloting indexed real polarization.)

- In 1948, the Mississippi and part of the Alabama delegation walked out of the Democratic convention over civil rights, paving the way for a third-party Dixiecrat ticket in November.

- In 1968, rioting in the streets of Chicago spilled into the Democratic convention, adding to a polarization that kept Eugene McCarthy, the losing candidate, from endorsing the winner, Hubert Humphrey, until late in the campaign.

- In 1972, the dominant McGovern faction at the Democratic convention refused to seat the Chicago machine delegation led by Mayor Richard Daley,

8. For one indicator showing the prominence of the party nominating conventions of 1896, see David R. Mayhew, *America's Congress: Actions in the Public Sphere, James Madison through Newt Gingrich* (New Haven: Yale University Press, 2000), 148–53.

thereby ousting an element that had been of central importance to the party since 1933.[9]

For the nineteenth century, this event inventory jibes quite well with the realignments calendar. The 1840s aside, the extreme combustibility of the 1860 and 1896 conventions makes for a good fit. But for the twentieth century, the "convention turmoil" hypothesis not only fails to fit well but is fundamentally misleading about the American system. In 1932 and 1936, notwithstanding the helplessness and rage brought on by the Great Depression, both the Republican and Democratic parties conducted their nominating conventions without suffering any significant integrative problems,[10] and, for that matter, they jointly managed to soak up almost all the popular vote during the elections of those years. It was a striking performance. By contrast, consider the last years of the Weimar Republic. An electoral realignment may have been going on in the United States in the early and mid-1930s, but nothing is more remarkable about the American parties of those years than their "integrative" capacities, in conventions and otherwise.

7) *Third parties*. Whatever their logics, the various theories connecting third-party eruptions to realignments

---

9. Most of the particulars in this paragraph are from *National Party Conventions, 1831–1980* (Washington, D.C.: Congressional Quarterly, Inc., 1983).

10. As they had done in 1928, also often seen as a realigning year.

have suggested that the former will tend to take place soon before the latter. This is the case with Sundquist's issue intrusion theory, Burnham's "protorealignment phenomenon" theory, and Beck's generational "ripeness" theory.

Given the evidence, is the proximity claim valid? Let it be said that, as a matter of statistical patterning, this idea comes closer to pay dirt than most other realignment ideas.[11] Consider the temporal extremes of the canonical realignment eras. At one extreme, all the closing segments of those eras have indeed exhibited such eruptions—the Know Nothings and much else in the 1850s, the Populists in the 1890s, and the La Follette Progressives in the 1920s. There are no yawning vacancies. At the other extreme, none of the chief opening segments—the late 1860s and 1870s, the 1900s, the 1930s and early 1940s—has exhibited any such eruption (or at least is widely believed to have done so; see below). Those are good results. They accord with theoretical predictions, and they are at least suggestive.

But then troubles set in. As it happens, several notable third-party eruptions have occurred *near the midpoints* of the alleged realignment eras, not during their closing phases—namely, the Liberty and Free Soil parties in the

11. Also particularly impressed by the third-parties evidence are Jerome Clubb, William H. Flanigan, and Nancy H. Zingale in their *Partisan Realignment: Voters, Parties, and Government in American History* (Beverly Hills, Calif.: Sage, 1970), 151–52.

1840s, the Greenback party in the late 1870s,[12] the Progressive and Socialist parties in 1912 (the Socialists hit their all-time peak that year), and possibly the Dixiecrats and Henry Wallace Progressives in 1948. This pattern is bad news for Beck's twenty-five-year "ripeness" idea; it raises the question of how long Burnham's "proto" should be allowed to precede "realignment," and, more generally, it makes one wonder whether an overall pattern of correspondence between third parties and realignments really exists. In particular, the election of 1912 is an embarrassing elephant in the living room.[13] Sixteen years after 1896, that election brought the largest third-party vote ever—27.4 percent for the Progressives led by Theodore Roosevelt—as well as a *fourth*-party vote of 6.0 percent for the Socialists that rivaled all by itself, say, the 8.5 percent won by the Populists in 1892.

To deal with this problem of off-schedule third parties, realignments advocates have made two moves. One is to designate a new phenomenon of "mid-sequence realignments," or "adjustments," falling in "periods of relatively high tension which are located about midway in the life cycle of an electoral era," at which times third parties play

12. According to Sundquist, the Greenback party peaked in the 1878 midterm election. James L. Sundquist, *Dynamics of the Party System: Alignment and Realignment of Political Parties in the United States* (Washington, D.C.: Brookings Institution, 1983), 113–14.

13. See, e.g., Clubb, Flanigan, and Zingale, *Partisan Realignment*, 143, fig. 4.4.

a role as "midpoint indicators of tension."[14] I have not come across a theoretical defense of this seemingly ad hoc idea. The other move is to discount the election of 1912. It was, according to Beck, "the result of a split within the ranks of the majority party over personalities rather than policies."[15] For other reasons—not for its off-schedule location—Burnham also discounts 1912. It featured a "major-party bolt" of little consequence rather than the kind of protest movement that points to a realignment.[16] Are these putdowns warranted? Granted, Theodore Roosevelt was a party bolter, but it is also true that the Progressive party of 1912 was an army of crusading reformers aiming for, among other things, national health insurance, social security, an inheritance tax, women's suffrage, government-led industrial planning, and popular override of judges.[17] These were not President Taft's priorities. Little of that era's reform agenda was overlooked. It is interesting that Key, in crafting a Sundquist-type argument about third parties, backed away from discounting 1912: "With respect to the policy orientations of the major parties, the minor-party eruptions in some instances nudge

14. Ibid., 26; Burnham, *Critical Elections and the Mainsprings*, 28–29.

15. Beck, "The Electoral Cycle," 138.

16. Burnham, *Critical Elections and the Mainsprings*, 27–28. Burnham does not mention the election of 1912 in this passage, but his meaning is clear enough.

17. See Sidney M. Milkis and Daniel J. Tichenor, "'Direct Democracy' and Social Justice: The Progressive Party Campaign of 1912," *Studies in American Political Development* 8 (1994), 282–340.

the major parties differentially and widen the policy gap between them. The years 1892, 1912, and 1924 appear to have been instances of this sort."[18]

As for the early parts of realignment eras being barren of third-party eruptions, that could use reconsideration. In the evolution of scholarship about third parties during the last half century, one surprise is the demotion of the Liberal Republicans of 1872. Once a staple item in the accounts,[19] they have become a footnote. What happened in 1872, twelve years after the critical election of 1860, is that the Republicans, led by President Grant, suffered an elite defection unmatched by any party since: the bolters included Charles Sumner, Charles Francis Adams, Lyman Trumbull, Carl Schurz, and George W. Julian, an all-star cast from the 1860s. A Liberal Republican convention nominated Horace Greeley for president against Grant. In a showing of passiveness unique for a major party in American history, the Democrats proceeded to nominate Greeley also. As a consequence, the Liberal Republicans, by failing to win any general-election votes distinctly their own, lost a chance to appear in future statistical

18. V. O. Key, Jr., *Politics, Parties, and Pressure Groups* (New York: Thomas Y. Crowell, 5th ed., 1964), 280.

19. See, e.g., V. O. Key, Jr., *Politics, Parties, and Pressure Groups* (New York: Thomas Y. Crowell, 1942), 280–82; Howard P. Nash, Jr., *Third Parties in American Politics* (Washington, D.C.: Public Affairs Press, 1959), ch. 5; Wilfred E. Binkley, *American Political Parties: Their Natural History* (New York: Knopf, 1959), 297–300.

calculations of third-party success. It is not clear how to deal with this 1872 eruption, but ignoring it is not the obvious option—in part because the regular Republicans' issue positioning four years later in 1876 seems to have drawn from it. Consider also the 1840s. The non-early appearances, by realignment era standards, of the Liberty and Free Soil parties of 1844 and 1848 owe entirely to a designation of 1828 as that era's break-point realignment date—a questionable choice. If that break point is shifted to 1836 or 1838 where it probably belongs, given that one is needed at all, the Liberty and Free Soil eruptions come to look precocious.

In the face of these various difficulties, skepticism is probably warranted about any overall correspondence between third-party eruptions and realignments. A less demanding view of third parties might be, as Key wrote in 1958: "From time to time questions not soluble by the intraparty processes of the major parties will arise and spill out into third party movements. Such matters have arisen at least in 1872, 1892, 1912, 1924, and 1948."[20] Today, we might add 1968 (George Wallace), 1980 (John Anderson), 1992 (Ross Perot), 1996 (Ross Perot), and 2000 (Ralph Nader). To fit these events to a realignments calendar is a daunting task. In the most impressive quantitative work on American third parties, by Steven J. Rosenstone,

20. V. O. Key, Jr., *Politics, Parties, and Pressure Groups* (New York: Thomas Y. Crowell, 4th ed., 1958), 309.

Roy L. Behr, and Edward H. Lazarus, distance from the last realignment is not one of the variables reported to be a predictor of size of third-party vote.[21] However, on the brighter side for the realignments genre, those authors report that the presence of "nationally prestigious third party candidates [like Theodore Roosevelt] on the ballot" *does* help to predict the size of the third-party vote, and distance from the last realignment does help to predict whether *that* happens.[22] The logic is that major politicians like Theodore Roosevelt and Martin Van Buren are not apt to bolt their parties until a generation or so after a realignment's passions and issues have died down. Again, on the dimmer side, however, that last finding is statistically precarious, it suffers from the 1828 malady, and its underpinning data points do not encourage the idea of a realignment in the 1890s.[23]

8) *Durable new issue cleavages.* Is it true that electoral

21. Steven J. Rosenstone, Roy L. Behr, and Edward H. Lazarus, *Third Parties in America: Citizen Response to Major Party Failure* (Princeton: Princeton University Press, 2d ed., 1996), 154. The Liberal Republicans of 1872 do not figure in this analysis.

22. Ibid., 139–42, 193, 201–3.

23. "Nationally prestigious" third-party presidential candidates include "current or former presidents and vice-presidents, as well as current or former U.S. senators, representatives, or governors who have [previously] run for president or vice-president within one of the major parties" (ibid., 140). The food for the variable is nine such candidates between 1840 and 1980 (141): Martin Van Buren (1848), Millard Fillmore (1856), John Breckinridge (1860), Theodore Roosevelt (1912), Robert La Follette (1924), Henry Wallace (1948), George Wallace (1968), Eugene McCarthy (1976), and John Anderson (1980).

realignments have been distinctively associated with new
and durable party cleavages over interests, ideological
tendencies, or issues? This is not an easy subject to get
hold of, and, in general, assertions about it have outpaced
measurement. So far as I am aware, the most sophisticated and convincing work of relevance is by John Gerring, who recently used some two thousand texts to code
rhetoric (including that in party platforms) emanating
from candidates and other party figures during presidential campaigns from 1828 through 1992.[24] Gerring looks
for "ideology," let it be noted, rather than, as in Sundquist's
case, "issues" or "clusters of related issues." The two objec-
tives are not identical. Yet Gerring's ideology does include
issues (at one point he unpacks the larger term to mean
"values, beliefs, and issue-positions"),[25] he provides time-
series data on certain issues that figure as ingredients of
ideologies, and at any rate, going by the Schattschneider
and Sundquist presentations as a whole, the term *ideology*
may cut as close to the joint as the terms *issue* or *cluster of
related issues*. In the case of the 1890s, consider Schattschneider's "radical" and "conservative" blocs[26] and Sundquist's roomy "inequality in the distribution of wealth and

24. John Gerring, *Party Ideologies in America, 1828–1996* (New York:
Cambridge University Press, 1998), 6 and appen.

25. Ibid., 6.

26. E. E. Schattschneider, *The Semisovereign People: A Realist's View of
Democracy in America* (New York: Holt, Rinehart, and Winston, 1960), 78–
82.

income among regions and classes" in that decade's new issue cluster.[27]

One result of Gerring's coding is a periodization of American party history—although the periods differ by party, they are unequal in length, and, he warns, they neither begin nor end quite as abruptly as their identifying dates might suggest. The periods are conveyed in his chapter titles that label epochs. For the Whigs and their successors the Republicans, 1828 through 1924 was the "National Epoch," whose rhetoric featured emphasis on *work* in the joint sense of the work ethic and free labor (the thrust was antislavery); *social harmony* as opposed to class conflict; *neomercantilism* in the form of government-led boosterism to promote economic growth as through tariffs; *statism* as a commitment to strong, guiding, authoritative government institutions; *order* in the face of, for example, late nineteenth-century anarchism and insurrections like that of 1861; *Yankee Protestantism* in an unending drive to promote moral correctness through government action, as with antislavery; and *nationalism* in the form of a triumphalist, integrative Americanism. The epoch's central theme, if there was one, was order over anarchy. At the level of individual issues, the protective tariff appeared prominently in Whig-Republican rhetoric from 1844 through 1852 and again from roughly 1884

27. Sundquist, *Dynamics of the Party System* (1983 ed.), 298–99.

through 1936 (spilling over into the next epoch). "Support for civil rights for African-Americans" (which accommodates antislavery positions) soared, unsurprisingly, in Republican rhetoric from 1856 through 1864, then sloped off at a lower level from 1868 into the early twentieth century. On this last issue, "it is important to note that civil rights dominated partisan discourse only during one brief period, immediately preceding and following the Civil War. Indeed, the banner under which Lincoln and other party leaders chose to conduct their campaigns—electoral and military—was the banner of nationalism. Republicans depicted themselves as protectors of the sacred Constitution and saviors of the union, not as protectors of black men and women."[28]

But then in the mid-1920s came a pivotal hinge for this grand old Republican party of order, statism, and government action. With Hoover and to some degree Coolidge leading the way, "the threat to liberty was reconceptualized; the danger was no longer anarchy, but rather the *state*. The federal government, for a century the party's ally, was now identified as a public enemy." Accordingly, a "Neoliberal Epoch" set in around 1928 that is still going strong today. The emphases came to be *antistatism*—the party's "long-standing and visceral dislike of big government . . . had its origins in the 1924 and 1928 cam-

28. Gerring, *Party Ideologies*. Caveats on periodization, 19; national epoch, 15–16 and ch. 3; tariff issue, 69; civil rights issue, 110.

paigns"; *free market capitalism; individualism;* and *right-wing populism* in the style of assailing Washington, D.C. In Gerring's judgment, this Republican turnaround in the 1920s was "the most fundamental rethinking of American conservatism since the acceptance of mass democracy by the New England Federalists." What caused it? That is not clear, although the aggressive exercise of federal government power by Democrats during World War I is one possibility.[29]

For the Democratic party, a "Jeffersonian Epoch" lasting from 1828 through 1892 accentuated *white supremacy* before and after the abolition of slavery; *antistatism* in the form of "virulent opposition to the federal government"; and *civic republicanism* in the sense of upholding a virtuous agrarian way of life against speculation, corruption, and other threatening, often government-connected intrusions.[30] Then, in an abrupt switch in the 1890s, a "Populist Epoch" was inaugurated by Bryan that lasted into the late 1940s. Newly emphasized were *democratic majoritarianism* to the end of allowing the people to confront power; an *antimonopoly* assault against economic elites— "More, perhaps, than any other single theme, antimonopoly rhetoric tied the party of Bryan, Wilson, [Al] Smith,

29. Gerring, *Party Ideologies*. State as enemy (125, italics in original); antistatism (140); neoliberal epoch in general (15–16 and ch. 4); 1920s turnaround (158); causation (157–58).

30. Ibid., 15, 17 and ch. 5 on the Jeffersonian Epoch; antistatism, 169.

Roosevelt, and Truman together in the first half of the twentieth century"; a call for *government action* of "a regulatory style and redistributive purpose found hitherto only outside the mainstream of American party politics"; and *Christian humanism* through a righteous, call-to-duty tone abundantly evident in the rhetoric of Bryan, Wilson, and Franklin Roosevelt—for example, in the latter's "money changers in the temple" locution. One summary of this epoch's rhetoric is "the people versus the interests."[31] The American business sector or Wall Street rather than, as earlier for the Jeffersonian Democrats, an actually or potentially oppressive state, kicked into place as the chief political menace, enemy, or target.[32] Gerring is emphatic on the idea of a "Bryan-Wilson-Roosevelt era." On the documentary evidence, "It was in 1896, not 1932, that the Democratic party first committed itself to a statist and redistributive vision of public policy."[33]

But that is not the end of the Democratic story. In Gerring's analysis, a new "Universalist Epoch" began for the party around 1952 that lasted into the 1990s. Emphasized

31. Ibid., 15–18 and ch. 6 on the Populist Epoch; quotations at 17, 189, 199. I have reworked Gerring's titles of themes associated with this epoch so as to supply a better fit, in my view, to the content of his Chapter 6. Quotation on presidents, 199; the "money changers" locution is from Roosevelt's first inaugural address.

32. On this 1890s juncture, see also James L. Huston, "The American Revolutionaries, the Political Economy of Aristocracy, and the American Concept of the Distribution of Wealth, 1765–1900," *American Historical Review* 98 (1993), 1079–1105, at 1102–5.

33. Gerring, *Party Ideologies*, 204, 229.

during this most recent epoch have been *civil rights, social welfare, redistribution,* and *inclusion*.[34] That is, around the middle of the twentieth century, once past Harry Truman's "give 'em hell" campaign of 1948, the Democratic party "discarded its abrasive, class-tinged ethos in favor of a *Universalist* perspective—the extension of rights to all aggrieved claimants and a general rhetoric of inclusion. Bryan, the evangelical crusader of the Populist era, was traded in for the moderate, ecumenical Lyndon Johnson. Party leaders now praised capitalism without qualification. Arguments for progressive social policies relied on empathy, social responsibility, and impassioned appeals for aid, rather than attacks on privilege and power. Postwar Democrats also reached beyond economic issues to address a wide range of 'postmaterialist' concerns."[35] Populism did occasionally surface again in the rhetoric of McGovern, Carter (in 1976), and Mondale, and in certain speeches in 2000 by Gore, who is otherwise a globalist and supported the North American Free Trade Agreement (NAFTA) in 2000, but it was recessive in Adlai Stevenson, Kennedy, Johnson, and Clinton. In general for the Democrats after 1950 or so: "Oppression and injustice were out;

34. On the Universalist Epoch, ibid., 17–18 and ch. 7.

35. Ibid., 18, italics in the original. On this mid-twentieth-century juncture, see also Alan Brinkley, *The End of Reform: New Deal Liberalism in Recession and War* (New York: Knopf, 1995). Brinkley documents the Democratic party elite's abandonment of "antimonopolyism" as a policy stance a bit earlier—in the late 1930s and early 1940s.

peace, harmony, and community were in. . . . It was a far cry from the Populist blame game."[36]

In these Gerring calculations, one clear bull's-eye emerges for the realignments perspective—the Bryanization of the Democratic party in the 1890s—and slavery and civil rights certainly did figure in the elections around 1860, but otherwise the fit is disappointing. At the level of particular issues or themes, slavery and civil rights gave way to other concerns in the 1870s and 1880s, raising a durability question about that issue.[37] At the level of ideologies, the realignments canon has no place for a Republican juncture in the 1920s or a Democratic juncture around 1950 (although recall my earlier case for a "party system" discontinuity during 1948 through 1956). And there is the unoriginality of the New Deal, which in Gerring's periodization is "more properly seen as an end

36. Gerring, *Party Ideologies,* 247. Is it an accident that both of Gerring's break points in party ideology during the twentieth century—the Republican one in the mid-1920s and the Democratic one around 1950—took place shortly after world wars? In the latter case, the astonishing, war-winning productivity of the basically private U.S. economy during World War II, the experience of cooperation among labor, management, and government during that war, and the lush—by past or European standards—postwar prosperity that continued through the late 1940s no doubt helped sidetrack the old antimonopoly critique of American capitalism. Bryanism was relegated to a left-wing fringe and academics. Also, the hypocrisy of waging a war against Nazism while accommodating racial discrimination at home became inescapable by the end of the war. That no doubt helped boost civil rights onto the postwar election agenda.

37. Ibid., 69, 77, 84, 94, 110.

point, rather than a starting point, in Democratic party ideology."[38]

Obviously, there are many ways of coding for issues or ideologies, and Gerring's work cannot close off all doubt or discussion about these matters. But it is the most impressive work so far on the content of party electoral appeals in American history; it goes out of its way to avoid anachronism—that is, a reading of today's organizing concepts into the past; and it stands as a challenge to realignments writers or anyone else who would periodize American electoral history.

This treatment of issues could rest here, but another consideration comes to mind. It raises a basic question about the nature of electoral politics. Ideologies as Gerring discusses them, or clusters of issues that might crystallize voter allegiances for thirty years or more as in the realignments canon, are likely to have a certain timeless quality. But in reality, how often is it that elections are fought and won over such long-lived constructs? A rather different picture can be drawn of American electoral history by centering on *events*—or on efforts by politicians to manage events. "Issue content" is still under scrutiny, but it is a content associated with something that has just recently happened.

38. Ibid., 229.

Here are some examples of event-driven issues in American history. Any of them could plausibly have affected the size (did a party gain over last time because of it?) or the mix (were alliances reshuffled because of it?) of existent voter coalitions in a distinctive way.

- In 1844: In light of various recent maneuvering, should Texas be annexed?
- In 1854: What should be the reaction to the Kansas-Nebraska Act?
- In 1860: After John Brown's raid on Harpers Ferry and the rest, what next? (According to one account, "There was a revolution of opinion in the South within six weeks after Harpers Ferry.")[39]
- In 1864: Which should it be—clear-cut military victory with Lincoln or a muddling compromise with McClellan?
- In 1866: How tough should Reconstruction policy be?
- In 1890: Have the Republicans gone overboard with their spending and regulatory schemes—notably the McKinley Tariff—in the so-called "billion-dollar Congress" under Benjamin Harrison?
- In 1894: Have the Democrats ruined the economy?
- In 1920: After two years of economic turmoil, fright-

39. David M. Potter, *The Impending Crisis, 1848–1861* (New York: Harper and Row, 1976), 382.

ening strikes, a red scare, and international revolution, which party is a better bet for order?

- In 1932: Who can get the economy working again?
- In 1934: Who *did* get the economy working again?
- In 1938: After two years of sitdown strikes in the auto plants, FDR's court-packing plan, allegations of Communists in the agencies, and another alarming economic downturn, is it time to curb the New Dealers?
- In 1944: Who can finish off the war better?
- In 1950, as McCarthyism crested: Should the left wing be purged? That classic election season brought defeat for Democratic Senators Claude Pepper of Florida (then sometimes called "Red Pepper"), Frank Graham of North Carolina, Glen Taylor of Idaho (the running mate of Henry Wallace in 1948), Elbert Thomas of Utah, and Millard Tydings of Maryland (who was not a left-winger or even a liberal but had gotten on the wrong side of McCarthy), Vito Marcantonio, the veteran American Labor Party congressman from New York, and Senate aspirant Helen Gahagan Douglas in the so-called "pink lady" campaign in California.[40]

40. The Pepper, Graham, and Taylor defeats occurred in Democratic primaries. On Pepper: Tracy E. Danese, *Claude Pepper and Ed Ball: Politics, Purpose, and Power* (Gainesville: University of Florida Press, 2000), ch. 9. On

- In 1952: Is Eisenhower the remedy for "Communism, corruption, and Korea" (the GOP slogan that year)?
- In 1968: What is the remedy for rioting in the cities and a quagmire war?
- In 1974 and 1976: After Watergate, who can be trusted?
- In 1994: Can the grand domestic policy plans of the Clinton administration be trusted?
- In 1998: Should Clinton be evicted from office?[41]

There is no way to prevent voters, politicians, or parties from dwelling on event-centered issues like the foregoing. Indeed, any democratic system that tried to do so—imagine a requirement that voters make decisions only by consulting party stances or cleavages of a sort that might

---

Graham: Julian M. Pleasants and Augustus M. Burns III, *Frank Porter Graham and the 1950 Senate Race in North Carolina* (Chapel Hill: University of North Carolina Press, 1990). On Taylor: Boyd A. Martin, "The 1950 Elections in Idaho," *Western Political Quarterly* 4 (1951), 75–81. On Thomas: Frank H. Jonas, "The Art of Political Dynamiting," *Western Political Quarterly* 10 (1957), 374–91. On Tydings: Caroline H. Keith, *"For Hell and a Brown Mule": The Biography of Senator Millard E. Tydings* (Lanham, Md.: Madison, 1991), chs. 1, 2; David M. Oshinsky, *A Conspiracy So Immense: The World of Joe McCarthy* (New York: Free Press, 1983), 174–76. On Marcantonio: Reinhard H. Luthin, *American Demagogues: Twentieth Century* (Boston: Beacon Press, 1954), ch. 9, at 232–34. On Douglas, then a member of the U.S. House: Greg Mitchell, *Tricky Dick and the Pink Lady: Richard Nixon vs. Helen Gahagan Douglas, Sexual Politics and the Red Scare, 1950* (New York: Random House, 1998).

41. See Alan I. Abramowitz, "It's Monica, Stupid: The Impeachment Controversy and the 1998 Midterm Election," *Legislative Studies Quarterly* 26 (2001), 211–26.

last for thirty years—would probably collapse through rendering its elections irrelevant.

In summary, in the realm of long-term issue cleavages, the realignments perspective runs into questions of both validity (is the periodization correct?) and illuminative power (how much of politics and policy making can be accounted for by any kind of long-term issue cleavage?).

9) *Ideological polarization.* At issue here is a Burnham claim: at realignment junctures, an "insurgents' political style" that is "exceptionally ideological by American standards" brings on an atypical level of "ideological polarization" between the parties.[42] Has this actually happened? A decisive answer would require two metrics, not just one—a measure of ideological style and a measure of polarization. Of relevance for the former might be, for example, whether a party's stance tends exceptionally toward "visionary theorizing" or "a systematic body of concepts," to borrow two dictionary phrases,[43] or toward "highly salient issue-clusters, often with strongly emotional and symbolic overtones," to cite Burnham.[44] In

42. Walter Dean Burnham, "Party Systems and the Political Process," ch. 10 in William N. Chambers and Burnham (eds.), *The American Party Systems: Stages of Political Development* (New York: Oxford University Press, 1967), 288; Burnham, *Critical Elections and the Mainsprings*, 7.

43. *Webster's New Collegiate Dictionary*, 1977 ed., s.v. "ideology."

44. Burnham, *Critical Elections and the Mainsprings*, 7. Note that the term *ideology* as used here means style as opposed to, in Gerring's case, substantive content. Here, a party's stance might in principle be graded high, medium, or low according to how ideological its style is; in Gerring's

principle, "polarization" is the distance between the two major parties' stances at any election.

To my knowledge, neither of these two values has been convincingly indexed across American electoral history. Should good measures ever come to exist, another problem would very likely emerge: one value would not map anywhere near perfectly onto the other. The election of 1860, for example, would probably fly off the charts for polarization, but on casual evidence it does not seem to have been particularly ideological. In the face of these difficulties, a little probing at the edges drawing on casual knowledge is the only practical option, and I will give it a try.

Leaving aside earlier eras, here is my take on this claim: it captures the 1890s reasonably enough, but it founders in the twentieth century. Its chief embarrassment is the election of 1932. Realigning though that contest may have been, it is an exceptionally unpromising place to look for an "insurgent's ideological style." To win in that terrible Depression year, all the Democrats needed to do was offer new management, and that in effect is what they did. According to William E. Leuchtenburg, "Roosevelt's platform, drafted at the Governor's request by A. Mitchell Palmer, was a conservative document. . . . The convention made only modest changes. In its final form,

_____

case, all party stances are equal in having a substantive content that can be coded for its thematic particulars.

the Democratic platform differed little from that of the Republican on economic questions, although the Democrats espoused somewhat more ambitious welfare programs."[45] As the Democratic candidate in 1932, Franklin Roosevelt ran a vague, please-all-sides campaign in which Hoover drew criticism for not having balanced the budget.[46]

Is the 1936 election a better bet for insurgent's ideological style, if Roosevelt could still be considered an insurgent then? Probably it is; a level of left-liberal rhetoric did emanate from Roosevelt during that campaign. Yet Truman arguably topped that in 1948,[47] and, more generally, what would an antiseptic search for insurgent political styles during the twentieth century turn up? One guess is that the standard setters would be Theodore Roosevelt's candidacy as a Progressive in 1912 (he probably deserves consideration since the Progressives finished second that year),[48] Barry Goldwater's candidacy in 1964, and George McGovern's in 1972. The latter two have been characterized by Benjamin I. Page as exactly "insurgent candidates. They won their parties' nominations with issue-oriented appeals and with the help of dedicated

45. William E. Leuchtenburg, *Franklin D. Roosevelt and the New Deal, 1932–1940* (New York: Harper and Row, 1963), 8–9. As Wilson's Attorney General, Palmer had presided over the "Red Scare" of 1919.

46. Ibid., 8–13.

47. In actual voting behavior, 1948 was the standout "class cleavage" election between 1936 and 1960; 1936 was just average for that time span. See Robert R. Alford, *Party and Society* (Chicago: Rand McNally, 1963), 227.

48. See Milkis and Tichenor, "'Direct Democracy' and Social Justice."

bands of activists."[49] Franklin Roosevelt even in 1936 looks like a resolute pragmatist in this company.

"Polarization," ideological or otherwise, is an elusive subject. Yet whatever else was going on politically in the 1930s—and of course much was—it is not clear that polarization between the parties hit a maximum then. That doubt holds for 1936 as well as 1932.[50] The Republicans' nominee in 1936, Alf Landon, the kind of Republican who had backed Theodore Roosevelt for president in 1912 and Robert La Follette in 1924,[51] came into the 1936 campaign having "endorsed in general terms the stated general purposes of the New Deal, confining his criticisms to detail and method"[52]—including on the subject of federal old-age pensions, which he backed in principle.[53] The vice presidential nominee, Frank Knox, was an old Bull

49. Benjamin I. Page, *Choices and Echoes in Presidential Elections: Rational Man and Electoral Democracy* (Chicago: University of Chicago Press, 1978), 52.

50. On the Landon campaign in 1936, see Arthur M. Schlesinger, Jr., *The Politics of Upheaval* (Boston: Houghton Mifflin, 1960), 523, chs. 29 and 33, and 635–38; George H. Mayer, *The Republican Party, 1854–1966* (New York: Oxford University Press, 1967), 440–42; Leuchtenburg, *Franklin D. Roosevelt and the New Deal*, 175–79; James MacGregor Burns, *Roosevelt: The Lion and the Fox* (New York: Harcourt, Brace, 1956), 270–87; Kenneth S. Davis, *FDR: The New Deal Years, 1933–1937: A History* (New York: Random House, 1979), 623–27, 643–45.

51. Schlesinger, *The Politics of Upheaval*, 533; Mayer, *The Republican Party*, 430; Burns, *Roosevelt*, 270; Davis, *FDR*, 625.

52. Davis, *FDR*, 625.

53. Schlesinger, *The Politics of Upheaval*, 613–14.

Mooser.[54] Landon and the party's managers took pains to distance themselves from the intensely anti–New Deal Liberty League and the discredited Hoover.[55] As for the 1936 platform: "The Republicans, eyeing the great prize of the presidency and the obvious appeal of New Deal prosperity and reform, enunciated a moderately liberal platform."[56] Roosevelt, for his part, attacked the Republicans for their "me-too" speeches.[57] It is true that conservative shrillness broke out late in the campaign as the recently enacted blueprint for financing Social Security came under attack,[58] but all in all, in the uphill circumstances of 1936, the Republicans seem to have been doing their best to court the median voter as the Downsian model would instruct.[59]

At least the following conclusion seems warranted: a winning case for the 1930s as an outlier instance of insurgent-led ideological polarization between the parties would require some convincing evidence. On the

54. Davis, *FDR*, 625.

55. Schlesinger, *The Politics of Upheaval*, 523, 605; Mayer, *The Republican Party*, 442; Leuchtenburg, *Franklin D. Roosevelt and the New Deal*, 179.

56. Burns, *Roosevelt*, 270.

57. Ibid., 280.

58. The Social Security financing scheme was a campaign magnet. Opposition failure to attack it, given its sequence of upfront payroll taxes starting in 1937 but no pension checks until 1942, would have been a considerable surprise.

59. Anthony Downs, *An Economic Theory of Democracy* (New York: Harper and Row, 1957).

polarization question taken alone, the elections of the 1930s would need to stand up against those offering, for example, Johnson versus Goldwater in 1964, Nixon versus McGovern in 1972, and Carter versus Reagan in 1980.

10) *National, not local issues.* Have realignment junctures been distinctively dominated by "national" issues? That could hardly be claimed of elections at the presidential level, since the presidency enjoys the whole nation as its constituency; all presidential elections offer national issues. (Although, oddly, if one seriously searched the history of presidential contests for those with localistic aspects, the 1896 election might rank high. In that year, a set of geographically concentrated special-interest tails—the silver industry as well as cotton and high-plains farmers— managed to wag the huge Democratic dog.)

But how about U.S. House elections? The point is important for David W. Brady, since a switch to "national rather than local issues" during realigning elections, he writes, has generated party mandates enabling Congress to overcome its alleged chronic problems of "inertia" and "incrementalism" in the policy realm.[60] But whether House elections have actually sorted this way is an empirical question—it cannot be settled by assertion or deduction—and, unfortunately, no authoritative measure ex-

60. David W. Brady, *Critical Elections and Congressional Policy Making* (Stanford: Stanford University Press, 1988), 12, 14.

ists to supply an answer. But the case for singling out the House elections of 1854–60, 1894, and 1932 as distinctively national is far from clear-cut.[61] For one thing, the elections of 1894 and 1932 (and also 1930) were classic instances of elections centering on "nationwide states of affairs"—that is, a poor economy everywhere favored the party not controlling the White House. That situation no doubt makes for national issues of a sort, yet a good many other House elections have borne, if to a lesser degree, the same profile of a poor economy plus adverse voter reaction—in recent decades, for example, those of 1938, 1958, 1974, 1980, and 1982.

Beyond this, if one scans impressionistically for manifest "national" issue content in House elections of the past, other elections spring up. In the historical vicinity of 1894, for example, why should 1894 be said to dominate 1874, which featured Reconstruction issues as well as a poor economy;[62] or 1890, which brought an immense national seat swing in reaction to, among other things, the newly enacted McKinley Tariff;[63] or 1910, with its Progressive

61. On those elections, see ibid., 33, 61–63, 91.

62. See William Gillette, *Retreat from Reconstruction, 1869–1879* (Baton Rouge: Louisiana State University Press, 1979), ch. 10; Eric Foner, *Reconstruction: America's Unfinished Revolution, 1863–1877* (New York: Harper and Row, 1988), ch. 11; Michael W. McConnell, "The Forgotten Constitutional Moment," *Constitutional Commentary* 11 (1994), 115–44, at 124–25.

63. See Harold U. Faulkner, *Politics, Reform, and Expansion: 1890–1900*

insurgency?[64] In fact, the contests of 1874, 1890, and 1910 all possibly outrank that of 1894 if "position issues" are considered—that is, issues where party A offers a program and party B offers an opposing program, rather than ones where an incumbent party gets hammered because the economy is weak. The evidence is soft, yet the case for House elections as emblematically national at the alleged realigning junctures is certainly unproven and probably weak.

In sum, none of the process or issue considerations discussed in this chapter bear out the realignments calendar very well. Suitable time-series patterns fail to appear for voter turnout, nominating turmoil, third parties, new issue cleavages, ideological polarization, or nationalization of issues.

(New York: Harper and Bros., 1959), 112–18; R. Hal Williams, *Years of Decision: American Politics in the 1890s* (New York: Wiley, 1978), 41, 44–45, 52–53; Edward Stanwood, *American Tariff Controversies in the Nineteenth Century*, vol. 2 (Boston: Houghton Mifflin, 1903), 287–95.

64. See George E. Mowry, *The Era of Theodore Roosevelt, 1900–1912* (New York: Harper and Bros., 1958), 266–68, 272–73; John Milton Cooper, Jr., *Pivotal Decades: The United States, 1900–1920* (New York: Norton, 1990), 160–63; Andrew E. Busch, *Horses in Midstream: U.S. Midterm Elections and Their Consequences, 1894–1998* (Pittsburgh: University of Pittsburgh Press, 1999), 84–87.

Policies and Democracy

ULTIMATELY FOR THE REALIGNMENTS genre, payoff territory arrives with its ambitious claims about policy making and its soaring assertions about American democracy and the "System of 1896." I address these topics in this chapter, beginning with the three claims introduced earlier about policy making. The genre divides on whether on-schedule policy making is a consequence of electoral realignments or, alternatively, a defining property of them, but that question need not detain us here.

11) *Major policy innovations*. Does a pattern exist, as David W. Brady claims, in which electoral realignments have ushered in "major shifts in public policy" or

"outpourings of new comprehensive public policies"?[1] No one doubts the policy fertility of the 1860s, which brought major innovations in education, transportation, banking and currency, homesteading, taxation, and tariff protection during the Civil War as well as that era's well-known burst of Reconstruction legislation after the war. No one would question the 1930s, with its First and Second New Deals in 1933 and 1935. But how about the 1890s? Not then, wrote Schattschneider,[2] and Burnham, in his more recent writings, agrees: "The realignment of 1894–1896 *did not* result in a major reversal of dominant public policy."[3]

This is the third rail of the realignments genre. It has been unwise to touch it.[4] In the legislative sphere, policy innovations under McKinley during 1897–1901 probably

1. David W. Brady, *Critical Elections and Congressional Policy Making* (Stanford: Stanford University Press, 1988), 18, vii.

2. E. E. Schattschneider, "United States: The Functional Approach to Party Government," 194–215, in Sigmund Neumann (ed.), *Modern Political Parties: Approaches to Comparative Politics* (Chicago: University of Chicago Press, 1956), 197–98.

3. Walter Dean Burnham, "Periodization Schemes and 'Party Systems': The 'System of 1896' as a Case in Point," *Social Science History* 10 (1986), 263–313, at 269; italics in original. See also Burnham, "The System of 1896: An Analysis," ch. 5 in Paul Kleppner et al., *The Evolution of American Electoral Systems* (Westport, Conn.: Greenwood, 1981), 175.

4. As does Brady in *Critical Elections and Congressional Policy Making*, at vii, 17, 18, 53, 75–83, 121–24, 126–27. Still, on the plus side, Brady performed a service by at least pursuing the question of policy payoffs. Absent such payoffs as an ingredient, it is not clear that the realignments genre would ever have commanded much interest.

rank in the bottom quartile among all presidential terms in American history. Two enactments are ordinarily mentioned.[5] One is the important Dingley Tariff of 1897, although note that a party oscillation model well short of realignment theory can account for that measure. The Republicans had a custom of raising tariff duties whenever they captured complete control of the federal government—they did it in 1861 and 1890 and would do it again in 1922—just as the contrary-minded Democrats used such victories to lower the duties in 1894 and again in 1913 and 1934.[6] The second measure is the Gold Standard Act of 1900, but how much of an innovation was that? In fact, zealous support for gold had carried down from the Democratic Cleveland administration (they, not the party's Bryan faction, had been running the country) through the McKinley Republicans. "The existing gold standard must be maintained," exhorted the Republican platform of 1896, and it was.[7]

5. E.g., in Lawrence H. Chamberlain, *The President, Congress and Legislation* (New York: Columbia University Press, 1946). Strictly speaking, Chamberlain also mentions the Militia Act of 1901, enacted in the last days of McKinley's first term in 1901, as the first of three army reform statutes levered by Secretary of War Elihu Root.

6. There is one exception to this generalization between 1854 and 1952. The Republicans ascended to complete (if tenuous) control of the federal government in the 1880 election without raising the tariff.

7. Kirk H. Porter and Donald Bruce Johnson (compilers), *National Party Platforms, 1840–1960* (Urbana: University of Illinois Press, 1961), 108. More

Brady presses for two other realignment-induced policy innovations during 1897–1901. One is that era's "rise
of expansionism" in U.S. foreign policy, which seems a
stretch.[8] Expansionist spirit had pervaded the entire decade of the 1890s as Benjamin Harrison's administration
expanded the navy and risked war with Chile, and Grover
Cleveland's administration provoked a crisis with Britain
over Venezuela.[9] Also, the Spanish-American War waged
by the reluctant McKinley had its own well-known on-the-
spot etiology in 1898: it scarcely enjoyed a basis in the
election campaign of 1896 like those enjoyed by, say, the
War of 1812 in the campaign of 1810, the Mexican War in
that of 1844, or the Civil War in that of 1860. Stanley L.
Jones has remarked on that 1896 recessiveness: "Foreign
policy issues, too, were almost totally submerged by the
debate over free silver. . . . On most of these foreign policy
issues [Hawaii, Cuba, Venezuela where the Democrats
had been out front] public opinion and party positions
were not sharply defined. . . . The people were more inter-

specifically, the pledge was to maintain that standard short of an "international agreement with the leading commercial nations of the earth" to coin
silver freely, which the party promised to promote. Such an agreement was
not a likely prospect.

    8. Brady, *Critical Elections and Congressional Policy Making*, 53, 76–77,
at 76.

    9. See John M. Blum et al., *The National Experience: A History of the
United States* (New York: Harcourt Brace Jovanovich, 1981), ch. 21 ("Empire
Beyond the Seas").

ested in other issues in 1896, and none of the principals in the campaign saw any advantage for himself in diverting their attention to foreign policy."[10]

Brady's other innovation is an alleged surge in congressional appropriations under McKinley, on the theoretical ground that "the [House] Appropriations Committee will appropriate nonincremental amounts during realignments to fund new programs."[11] Agriculture is exhibited as an example.[12] But in fact, agriculture appropriations had grown four times as fast under the previous Republican president, Harrison, in 1889–93 (from $1.7 million to $3.2 million), as they did under McKinley in 1897–1901 (from $3.3 million to $4.0 million).[13] (The comparison with Harrison seems apt since the Republicans of the late nineteenth century, unlike the Democrats through Cleveland, had a tradition of favoring activist government.)[14] To take the pairs of bracketing dates again, federal outlays in general—minus those for the Department of War, which

10. Stanley L. Jones, *The Presidential Election of 1896* (Madison: University of Wisconsin Press, 1964), 335–36.

11. Brady, *Critical Elections and Congressional Policy Making*, 17; see also 119–27.

12. Ibid., 125–27.

13. *Statistical Abstract of the United States*, 1896, Docs C18.14: 1896, p. 15; *Statistical Abstract of the United States, 1902*, Docs C18.14: 1902, p. 36. Considering data for deficiency appropriations for agriculture for the relevant times does not significantly affect the calculations.

14. See, e.g., Robert S. Salisbury, "The Republican Party and Positive Government: 1860–1890," *Mid-America* 68 (1986), 15–34.

ballooned during the Spanish-American War—grew by 30.6 percent under Harrison but only 19.9 percent under McKinley.[15]

In the vicinity of the 1890s, Congresses can easily be found that were more innovative than either of McKinley's taken alone or even together. Under Harrison in 1889–91, the Republicans generated the McKinley Tariff (McKinley was a House member then), the aforementioned naval expansion, the Sherman Antitrust Act, the Sherman Silver Purchase Act, and an expansion of Civil War pensions broad enough to help fuel discussion recently about a late nineteenth-century American welfare state.[16] (These pensions were the chief ingredient of the spending surge under Harrison.) Under Theodore Roosevelt in 1905–7 came a bustle of regulatory activity—the Pure Food and Drug Act and the lengthily deliberated Hepburn Act regulating the railroads.[17] Either of Wilson's first-term Congresses of 1913–15 and 1915–17 would qualify. "Policy inertia," to draw a contrast, is the term used by historian Richard L. McCormick to characterize the years following the elec-

15. United States Bureau of the Census, *Historical Statistics of the United States, Colonial Times to 1970* (Washington, D.C.: U.S. Government Printing Office, 1975), vol. 2, 1114.

16. Theda Skocpol, *Protecting Soldiers and Mothers: The Political Origins of Social Policy in the United States* (Cambridge: Harvard University Press, 1992), ch. 2. On the Congress of 1889–91 in general, see Ernest S. Bates, *The Story of Congress 1789–1935* (New York: Harper and Bros., 1936), 300–305.

17. On the Hepburn Act, see Jeffrey K. Tulis, *The Rhetorical Presidency* (Princeton: Princeton University Press, 1987), ch. 4.

tion of 1896,[18] and that traditional understanding of those years is probably best left intact.

Faced by this legislative meagerness, Burnham has reached for the business-friendly federal judiciary, as opposed to the legislative process, as the relevant policy-making arena of an alleged 1894–1937 "integrated era."[19] However true that may be, the claim at issue here involves policy *change*. Did the federal courts supply it? At the least, given the sense of the realignments interpretation about the direction of policy change associated with the McKinley era, it would have to be shown that the judiciary was significantly more hostile to the business community during the generation before the 1896 realignment than it was to become during the generation afterward. Burnham does not say or seem to imply that, and to demonstrate it would be a formidable task. In a search of reputable authors on this subject, I came across few who locate a notable judicial policy break point in the mid-1890s. For Robert G. McCloskey, the Supreme Court's "major value" throughout its entire "second great period of constitutional history"—1865 through 1937—was "the protection of the business community against government." The Court sought that goal incrementally through such

18. Richard L. McCormick, "Walter Dean Burnham and 'The System of 1896,'" *Social Science History* 10 (1986), 245–62, at 245.

19. Burnham, "Periodization Schemes and 'Party Systems,'" 269–74, at 272; Burnham, "Constitutional Moments," 2256, 2267–69.

vehicles as the *Wabash* railroad-regulation case in 1886, the *E. C. Knight* antitrust case in 1895, the *ICC* rate case in 1896, and the *Lochner* maximum-hours case in 1905.[20] Arthur E. Sutherland describes a similar period of 1870 through 1930—"Industrialization; and Control by Nation and State"—during which business interests scored major Supreme Court victories in, to cite the cases he dwells on, *Wabash* in 1886, the *Minnesota* rate case of 1890, and *Lochner* in 1905. (He does take up the *Pollock* income tax case of 1895 in a separate chapter.)[21] For Carl Brent Swisher, the Supreme Court's romance with the pro-business due process clause ran from the late 1880s into the 1930s.[22] For Alpheus T. Mason and William M. Beaney, a short span from the mid-1880s through 1890 seems to have brought especially important change in the Court's policies vis-à-vis the business community, partly as a surprising result of Court personnel turnover during that time.[23] In particular, Justices Melville W. Fuller and David J. Brewer came aboard as Cleveland and Harrison appointees in the late 1880s, gelling the Court's conserva-

20. Robert G. McCloskey, *The American Supreme Court* (Chicago: University of Chicago Press, 1960), chs. 5 and 6, at 104–5.

21. Arthur E. Sutherland, *Constitutionalism in America: Origin and Evolution of Its Fundamental Ideas* (New York: Blaisdell, 1965), ch. 15; on *Pollock*, 333.

22. Carl Brent Swisher, *The Supreme Court in Modern Role* (Washington Square: New York University Press, 1958), 23–24.

23. Alpheus T. Mason and William M. Beaney, *The Supreme Court in a Free Society* (Englewood Cliffs, N.J.: Prentice-Hall, 1959), 34, 116–17, 151–52, 191, 227–31.

tive pro-business majority. From a realignments standpoint, that is the wrong decade.

In two works that do bound their analyses in the mid-1890s, the logic is still of a buildup of pro-business Court doctrines *before* that time. For Arnold M. Paul, a "new trend" evident in the *Minnesota* rate case of 1890 culminated in *E. C. Knight, Pollock,* and the *In re Debs* labor injunction case in 1895 during the second Cleveland administration.[24] For Alan F. Westin, an evolution of doctrines between 1876 and 1896 came to cast the Supreme Court, through the reactions it provoked, as a "midwife" of the Populist revolt.[25] Perhaps these two sources establish at least an 1890s "accentuation point," as opposed to a break point, in relevant Court doctrines. But that does not seem like fuel enough to propel the realignments machine, even accepting the surprising premise that judicial fuel might be used.

Which brings up another consideration: none of the sources cited above dwells on the electoral realignment of 1896 as a *cause* of change, accentuation, or even stasis in judicial policy making. As a theoretical matter, given the essentials of the realignments case, shouldn't that absence cause concern? Shouldn't it require serious evidence and

24. Arnold M. Paul, *Conservative Crisis and the Rule of Law: Attitudes of Bar and Bench, 1887–1895* (Ithaca: Cornell University Press, 1960), 39.
25. Alan F. Westin, "The Supreme Court, the Populist Movement, and the Campaign of 1896," *Journal of Politics* 15 (1953), 3–41, at 41.

argument to connect American judicial policy making in any way to a background electoral environment?[26] What was the connection, if any, for example, between the emergence of the Warren Court and the electoral environment of the 1950s? The absence of evidence for the 1890s seems to continue: in a search of Martin J. Sklar's relatively recent *Corporate Reconstruction of American Capitalism, 1890–1916: The Market, the Law, and Politics* for any sign of a causal path leading backward through judicial processes to the elections of 1894 or 1896, I came up with nothing.[27]

The 1890s pose a basic interpretive difficulty for the realignments genre. Policy change of turnaround dimensions favoring the business community is not to be found. The problem is the baseline. In the history of the world, when has a governmental environment ever favored private capitalism more than America did during the 1860s through the mid-1890s? There were many felicities—even

26. In this book, I have skirted a small, complicated literature addressing ties in general between electoral realignments and judicial decision making. Various ties have been proposed. One particularly rigorous work of recent vintage using a mass of data left its author disappointed: "The evidence . . . does not consistently support either the policy conflict role following critical elections or the agenda-setting role before critical elections." "It is, however, very difficult to ascribe a consistent role to Supreme Court policymaking across all realignments." John B. Gates, *The Supreme Court and Partisan Realignment: A Macro- and Microlevel Perspective* (Boulder, Colo.: Westview, 1992), 167, 174.

27. Martin J. Sklar, *The Corporate Reconstruction of American Capitalism, 1890–1916: The Market, the Law, and Politics* (New York: Cambridge University Press, 1988). Also, notice Sklar's periodization.

if some were hard-won or continually contested. On offer were high protective tariffs (on balance, they were arguably higher during 1861–96 than during 1897–1930),[28] solid property and contract rights, huge free land grants to the railroads, easy availability of an immigrant labor force from Europe, free trade across a continent, low taxes, a stable currency, little government regulation, and, in a pinch, presidents ready to send in federal troops to put down politicizing strikes, as in 1877 and 1894. How much more could be asked?

12) *Long spans of unified party control.* This overlaps the preceding claim. It is certainly true that the three chief alleged realignments have ushered in record spans of unified party control of the government—fourteen years apiece after the 1860, 1896, and 1932 elections. Since the 1830s, the runner-up is the ten-year span of Republican control after the 1920 election. But what are we to make of this information? Following Clubb, Flanigan, and Zingale, is it also true that such spans have outshone others in fostering "major policy innovations" that have become "embedded," "institutionalized," "assimilated," and less subject to "reversal and dismantlement"?[29]

28. See John Mark Hansen, "Taxation and the Political Economy of the Tariff," *International Organization* 44 (1990), 527–51, at 540.

29. Jerome M. Clubb, William H. Flanigan, and Nancy H. Zingale, *Partisan Realignment: Voters, Parties, and Government in American History* (Beverly Hills, Calif.: Sage, 1980), ch. 5, at 157, 160, 163. See also Walter Dean Burnham, Jerome M. Clubb, and William H. Flanigan, "Partisan Re-

This is a vast, not very well charted subject to which I shall try to bring some order. Consider first the long party-control spans cited above in light of three threshold evidence criteria. How well have those spans performed as producers of policy innovations that can be seen as major, durable, and at least plausibly linked to the specified generative elections?

Exquisite results are of course available for the New Deal and Civil War eras. During 1933 through 1938, Roosevelt and the New Deal Congresses launched a great many major policy innovations that were to become "embedded"—for example, in the areas of agricultural subsidies, labor-management relations, old-age pensions, the minimum wage, river-valley development (the Tennessee Valley Authority), rural electrification, reciprocal trade, countercyclical fiscal spending (which became a conscious policy in 1938), and the regulation of banking, securities trading, communication, and transportation. In the 1860s, the winning of the Civil War, which was a kind of policy achievement all by itself, became embedded in the Thirteenth Amendment, which abolished slavery, and, later, the Fourteenth Amendment, which defined a range of individual rights. Also, as recited earlier, the Republicans under Lincoln enacted what amounted to an up-

---

alignment: A Systemic Perspective," ch. 1 in Joel H. Silbey, Allan G. Bogue, and William H. Flanigan (eds.), *The History of American Electoral Behavior* (Princeton: Princeton University Press, 1978), 64–70.

dated version of the failed Whig domestic program of the 1840s—a protective tariff,[30] banking and currency reforms, homesteading, internal improvements (a transcontinental railroad), and this time subsidies to land-grant colleges.[31] These Whiggish initiatives were to enjoy the good fortune of becoming embedded.

But that is just about it for the posited time spans. For the post-1896 era, given its dearth of policy innovations even remotely traceable to its initiating realignment, a set of claims anything like the above would be fantasy. (So far as I am aware, no realignments advocate has risked crediting the Progressive-oriented innovations after 1905 like the Hepburn Act regulating the railroads or the Sixteenth Amendment authorizing an income tax to the mid-1890s realignment, notwithstanding the continuity of Republican party control through 1910.)[32] In effect, claim 12 does not unearth any significant embedded policy content beyond the 1860s and 1930s, which in a sense *generated* the

30. In fact, the Republicans jumped the gun with the Morrill Tariff in early 1861. That statute was enacted during the waning days of the Buchanan administration by a lame-duck Congress elected in 1858 of which the Democrats had controlled the Senate. But by this time the South's anti-tariff delegations had largely decamped from Washington, D.C.

31. For thumbnail sketches of policy innovation during the 1860s and 1930s, see David R. Mayhew, "Presidential Elections and Policy Change: How Much of a Connection Is There?" ch. 5 in Harvey L. Schantz (ed.), *American Presidential Elections: Process, Policy, and Political Change* (Albany: State University Press of New York, 1996), 159–60, 162–63.

32. The Sixteenth Amendment was ratified later, but it was proposed to the states for ratification by a Republican Congress under President Taft.

realignments genre and therefore can hardly serve as tests of it. The runner-up party-control span of 1921–30 under Harding, Coolidge, and Hoover scarcely stands out for its embedded policy innovations either, although a close analysis might actually elevate its early phase above the McKinley era.[33]

For contrast, how about major policy innovations destined to become embedded that were enacted *outside* the stipulated party-control time spans? That is, they were enacted under divided party control or else under unified party control lasting less than ten or twelve years. In fact, an immense share of American policy history falls into these categories, starting with Alexander Hamilton's banking and credit policies in 1790–91 and the Jay Treaty with England in 1795–96. Here are some later high points. After Reconstruction came the Pendleton Act, establishing a federal civil service in 1883, the Interstate Commerce Act in 1887, and the Sherman Antitrust Act in 1890.[34] Woodrow Wilson's years brought the statutory income tax, the inheritance tax, the Federal Reserve system, the Federal Trade Commission, and women's suffrage. After World War II came the Taft-Hartley Act in 1947 (which

33. This is suggested by the account in Chamberlain, *The President, Congress, and Legislation*.

34. For an account of the embedding of the Pendleton Act, see Stephen Skowronek, *Building a New American State: The Expansion of National Administrative Capacities, 1877–1920* (New York: Cambridge University Press, 1982), 64–82.

reworked the imperfectly embedded Wagner Act of 1935 and has governed labor-management relations for more than half a century since then); urban renewal in 1949 and 1954; the National Science Foundation in 1950; the federal highway program in 1956; disability insurance in 1956; the Public Accommodations Act in 1964; food stamps in 1964; Medicare in 1965; the Voting Rights Act in 1965; origins-blind immigration reform in 1965; clean air standards in 1970; clean water standards in 1972; Supplementary Security Income (SSI) in 1972; the Endangered Species Act in 1973; private pension regulation (ERISA) in 1974; campaign finance reform in 1974; the Earned Income Tax Credit (EITC) in 1975; airline deregulation in 1978; Reagan's tax cut in 1981; the Americans with Disabilities Act in 1990; and the North American Free Trade Agreement (NAFTA) in 1993. What could it mean to say that, aside from the stipulated party-control spans, "the only rival circumstance" for enacting landmark policy initiatives "seems to be an external military threat"?[35]

At the least, this anecdotal treatment raises questions about the Clubb, Flanigan, and Zingale claim. Yet it stops short of addressing a particularly interesting ingredient of that claim. It is an ingredient of conditionality: given a major policy initiative, does long-extended control of the government thereafter by the same party *raise the odds* of

35. Clubb, Flanigan, and Zingale, *Partisan Realignment*, 185n3.

its becoming embedded? One might imagine that the answer is yes, and possibly it is, yet this, too, is an empirical matter calling for investigation—although it is an inordinately difficult one to investigate.[36]

Again resorting to anecdotes, a cautionary signal goes up quickly. What is the American prototype for major policy initiatives *not* becoming effectively embedded? In a league by itself is the ambitious Reconstruction legislation of the 1860s and 1870s—the Civil Rights Act of 1866, the Fourteenth Amendment insofar as it applied to African-Americans in the South (it had other applications), the Fifteenth Amendment in its intended southern reach, the various Reconstruction Acts of 1867–68, the Enforcement Acts of 1870–72, and the Civil Rights Act of 1875 (enacted by a lame-duck Republican Congress elected in 1872). At the level of implementation, none of these instruments survived the political winds of the mid-

36. Entirely absent from the writings of the realignments genre, so far as I can tell, is any reference to one particular argument why an extended period of unified party control might be needed for either the enactment of policy initiatives or their "embedding." The argument is that the presidency, House, Senate, and Supreme Court operate on different political cycles and that it can take time and continuing pressure to harmonize them. Recently, Bruce Ackerman has employed that idea in *We the People: Foundations* (Cambridge: Harvard University Press, 1991). One reason for its absence in the realignments genre, I suspect, is that the presidency, House, and Senate had little trouble swinging into policy harmony in 1861, 1897, and 1933. In the 1930s, of course, it took the New Dealers a few years to tame the Supreme Court, partly because of the exceptional circumstance that no Court vacancies opened up for Franklin Roosevelt to fill during his first term. Only one other twentieth-century president, Carter, suffered that lack.

dle and late 1870s intact. Long-term unified party control proved to be of little or no help once it gave way in 1874.

These dismal results are a reminder that plenty of factors affect whether a policy initiative "takes" once it is enacted.[37] Following common sense, a list of such factors would no doubt include the level of support an initiative enjoyed at the start (for example, was its enacting coalition narrowly partisan or broadly nonpartisan?); the level of commitment written into the original enactment (which can be high with, for example, new trust funds)[38]; favorable or unfavorable election trends often falling short of switches in party control; whether times have changed (the New Deal's relief measures lost relevance in the defense economy of World War II); whether a new program builds a clientele; whether the federal courts make favorable rulings; and, perhaps most of all, whether a new initiative once set on the ground seems to work. In the end, all these factors and no doubt others may operate regardless of spans of party control. One result is that embedding failures can readily be spotted both outside and inside the stipulated party-control spans. The former would include the Tax Reform Act of 1986, whose celebrated compression of the rate schedule soon gave way to

37. A related discussion appears in William N. Eskridge, Jr., and John Ferejohn, "Super-Statutes," manuscript, 2001.

38. See the treatment in Eric M. Patashnik, *Putting Trust in the US Budget: Federal Trust Funds and the Politics of Commitment* (New York: Cambridge University Press, 2000).

widening again; the "community action program" part of Lyndon Johnson's antipoverty program of 1964, which was politically dead two years after enactment; and a ban on child labor enacted under Wilson that the Supreme Court struck down. During the stipulated time spans, embedding failures since Reconstruction would include Roosevelt's National Industrial Recovery Act (NIRA), which was staggering from ineffectiveness even before the Court struck it down in 1935; and the Farm Tenancy Act of 1937 and Wagner-Steagall Housing Act of 1937, whose prospects of becoming consequential faded after the anti–New Deal shift in the 1938 midterm election.

As for embedding successes, consider the Federal Reserve Act of 1913, the Voting Rights Act of 1965, Medicare in 1965, and the Americans with Disabilities Act of 1990. As unshielded by long-term party control as those initiatives were, was there ever a remote chance they would be reversed? Instances like these make one wonder about many of the New Deal initiatives. Was a fourteen-year shield of formal party control really necessary? It seems a good bet that the banking and securities reforms of Roosevelt's first Congress became quickly embedded. Social Security, enacted in 1935, went on to survive an election assault in 1936 and a Supreme Court ruling in 1937 and after that never had its existence seriously challenged again—although the path of its development remained up for grabs.[39] The New Deal agricultural crop programs were just briefly dented by an adverse Court ruling in 1936.[40] The minimum wage, once enshrined in the Fair Labor Standards Act of 1938, was hardly likely to be abandoned. But this is speculation. It is difficult to know. My guess is that there is *some* value to the idea of extended party control as an embedding aid—possibly as regards the Wagner Act between 1935 and 1947, for example?—but that it is a mistake to claim too much.

Where does this leave the discussion? To my mind, the capsule truth about major policy initiatives headed for "embedding" is that they have been generously sprinkled through American history with notable concentrations in the 1860s and 1930s. Secondary concentrations appear in the 1910s and the 1960s and 1970s—a reminder that major policy innovation can take place without realignments.[41] But we all learned this factual framework in

39. Martha Derthick, *Policymaking for Social Security* (Washington, D.C.: Brookings Institution, 1979), ch. 6 and 185–86; Edward D. Berkowitz, *America's Welfare State: From Roosevelt to Reagan* (Baltimore: Johns Hopkins University Press, 1991), ch. 3.

40. After that ruling, "agricultural regulation was reinstalled within *6 weeks*, following organized lobbying by farming interests." Barbara Alexander and Gary D. Libecap, "The Effect of Cost Heterogeneity in the Success and Failure of the New Deal's Agricultural and Industrial Programs," *Explorations in Economic History* 37 (2000), 370–400, at 370; italics in original.

41. See David R. Mayhew, *Divided We Govern: Party Control, Lawmaking, and Investigations, 1946–1990* (New Haven: Yale University Press, 1991), 143–44.

elementary school. The realignments genre has added nothing to it. Worse yet, it seems to have impeded our understanding of the subject in at least four ways. It has licensed young scholars to make claims about public policy formation that lack concreteness or grasp or both. It has fed a political science tendency to favor independent variables or explanatory theories over actual policy patterns at an exorbitant ratio. It has focused policy interest on the relatively barren 1890s. And it has deflected interest from junctures when significant policy change actually did occur, notably the Progressive era.[42] As Richard L. McCormick has written: "Between about 1905 and 1915 both the states and the nation enacted far-reaching economic and social legislation affecting practically every nook and cranny of American urban-industrial civilization." This was "one of the most significant and creative bursts of policymaking in United States history."[43]

13) *Redistributive policy.* Have the canonical realignments stood out in particular for fostering "redistributive" policy change? Again, no one would hesitate to associate redistributive policy innovation with the 1860s (consider the Thirteenth Amendment) or the 1930s. The case for the 1930s seems to grow even better as new work appears em-

42. As Sundquist for one does realize. See James L. Sundquist, *Dynamics of the Party System: Alignment and Realignment of Political Parties in the United States* (Washington, D.C.: Brookings Institution, 1983), 177.

43. McCormick, "Walter Dean Burnham and 'The System of 1896,'" 257.

phasizing that decade's prodigious relief efforts[44] and addressing the likely wealth-equalizing effects of various statutes.[45] But I am not aware of any serious work attributing notable redistributive policy change, in either a progressive or a regressive direction, to the alleged realignment of the 1890s. Tariff rates aside, there was little policy change after McKinley's election of any kind, after all.

Again, one cost of dwelling on alleged realignments can be neglect of alternative past junctures or eras that might be productively spotlighted. In the redistributive realm, a good candidate would seem to be the immense increase in federal revenue and spending associated with World War II and the Korean War that proved to be irreversible.[46]

That exhausts the discussion of policy patterns. Next is a claim of a unique kind that distinguishes the realignments case.

44. David M. Kennedy, *Freedom from Fear: The American People in Depression and War, 1929–1945* (New York: Oxford University Press, 1999), ch. 9; Edwin Amenta, *Bold Relief: Institutional Politics and the Origins of Modern American Social Policy* (Princeton: Princeton University Press, 1998), ch. 4; Edwin Amenta, Ellen Benoit, Chris Bonastia, Nancy K. Cauthen, and Drew Halfmann, "Bring Back the WPA: Work, Relief, and the Origins of American Social Policy in Welfare Reform," *Studies in American Political Development* 12 (1998), 1–56.

45. Carole Shammas, "A New Look at Long-Term Trends in Wealth Inequality in the United States," *American Historical Review* 98 (1993), 412–31, at 426–29.

46. Ibid., 426–29; Charles L. Schultze, "Is There a Bias Toward Excess in U.S. Government Budgets or Deficits?" *Journal of Economic Perspectives* 6 (1992), 25–43; Robert Higgs, *Crisis and Leviathan: Critical Episodes in the Growth of American Government* (New York: Oxford University Press, 1987), ch. 2.

14) *The electorate weighs in effectively and consequentially at realignment junctures, but not otherwise.* "Approximately once in a generation"—at the canonical realignment junctures, that is—"vitally important contributions to American political development" are made.[47]

This is a large claim and, I believe, a mistaken one. It is a basic theoretical error to associate *changes* in November voting alignments (however lasting they may be) with the perspicacity of, level of concern underlying, effectiveness of, or consequentiality of decisions by the electorate. As long as parties cater to the electorate, or else emanate from it—as have American parties, with their highly participatory nominating processes (even before the coming of direct primaries)—any "contributions" that the electorate wishes to make are likely to nose their way into elections regardless of whether those elections feature realigning patterns. For one thing, if *both* major parties accommodate a proposed innovation, it may come to dominate policy making without any disturbance at all of received electoral patterns. If, say, in the 1880s, the bulk of Americans had suddenly decided that the country should officially convert to Islam, that idea might have been embraced by both parties in an election campaign and then

47. Walter Dean Burnham, "Party Systems and the Political Process," ch. 10 in William N. Chambers and Burnham (eds.), *The American Party Systems: Stages of Political Development* (New York: Oxford University Press, 1967), 287.

adopted as government policy without any electoral re-alignment.[48] That would have been a major voter contribution. But also, if both parties come to embrace an eyes-open public decision reflected in electoral processes to *reject* a proposed innovation, that is in principle no less a voter contribution. In the 1880s, for example, the pro-Islam forces might have caused a nationwide commotion by contesting the nominating processes of both parties in every state yet might have ended up dominating neither. (In historical fact, the latter model fits rather well the intrusion of the Second Ku Klux Klan into both parties' processes at the state and local levels in the 1920s.)

This may sound like the kind of abstract theorizing it is always easy to dream up and then dismiss, but the basic idea is both open to evidence and nontrivial. What are the evidence requirements? To capture developments like either kind of Islamic intrusion, voting data from general elections would obviously be insufficient. A range of phenomena would need investigating: changes in the direction and intensity of public opinion on relevant matters, possibly social-movement activity, interaction between voters and elites, voter behavior in nominating processes, strategies by candidates in nominating processes, strategies by parties in general elections. Elections would need to be approached as complicated social events sprawling

48. Sundquist, in a discussion of nonrealignments, is very good on this logic. See *Dynamics of the Party System* (1973), 11–18.

across months, possibly years—not just as renditions of November votes. Perhaps this point is obvious, but since the Islamic kind of intrusion does have a counterfactual aspect to it, I want to hammer home the idea that, finally, occurrences like this have to be a matter of evidence. Many electoral seasons could be exhaustively investigated without coming across anything like an Islamic intrusion.

As for nontriviality, at least one interesting point is at stake: Is wrenching, closely fought conflict—consider Burnham's ideological polarizations or Sundquist's sharp new issue cleavages—the only significant way for publics or electorates to exercise influence through elections? Why should we accept that? What is wrong with the idea of publics reaching at least some important decisions more or less consensually and injecting them into electoral processes? Or, as a variant, the idea of publics reaching certain important decisions more or less consensually *during* electoral processes, through interaction with elite political actors, and having those decisions count?

Are there elections that can serve as examples? A canvass should not be restricted to ones with issue menus that might last for thirty years. Consider the election of 1940. Against a background of France falling to the Nazis in May and June and Britain imperiled, the Republicans opted in an open nominating process for a nonisolationist candidate (the surprising Wendell Willkie) without suffering serious defections then or afterward, and the

Willkie-versus-Roosevelt November election, notwith-standing certain marginal late-season fudging by both sides, came to be readable as a victory for international-ism. How many election outcomes have been more impor-tant than that?

Or take the election of 1948, which channeled or evoked at least three highly important voter judgments that seem to have been hegemonic, let us say, if not ex-actly consensual.[49] The heart of the domestic New Deal was confirmed once again as Thomas E. Dewey won the Republican nomination with a "me-too" stance. Civil rights emerged as a winning issue for the first time since 1872 as the Democrats, outbidding the generally pro–civil rights Republicans on that front, won the White House despite a threatening third-party defection by their Dixie-crat element under Strom Thurmond that ultimately drew only 2.4 percent of the vote and four deep-southern states. And the government's new stance of Cold War inter-nationalism was triumphantly ratified. On the Republican side, both Dewey and Harold Stassen took an interna-tionalist position that seemed to resonate in the presiden-tial primaries. On the left, the anti–Cold War challenge by former Vice President Henry Wallace, conducted by the

49. For recent treatments, see Zachary Karabell, *The Last Campaign: How Harry Truman Won the 1948 Election* (New York: Knopf, 2000); Gary A. Donaldson, *Truman Defeats Dewey* (Lexington: University Press of Ken-tucky, 1999).

Progressive party against an unpromising background of the Berlin blockade, spiraled down to a humiliating result of no states and, as with Thurmond, 2.4 percent of the vote. All in all, it would be something of an insult to the voters of 1948 to argue that they could not have been making a "contribution" just because they neglected to realign themselves.

Approached in this way, the elections of 1940 and 1948 and probably several others would stand up against, say, that of 1896 as instances of effective and consequential voter expression.

Finally, there is the direct historical claim.

15) *The "System of 1896."* In line with the realignments interpretation, was the American business community "insulated" from "mass pressures" by a "System of 1896" for more than a third of a century?

Probably not. First of all, as argued earlier, there is the problem of contingency. In any reasonably open polity operating in an event-packed world, no election result can program the future like that. Not to be overlooked is that Republican control of the national government crumbled in 1910 and 1912. In a development ordinarily skimped on by realignments writers (although not by Sundquist) as an off-schedule intrusion, Progressive-oriented Democrats came to power under Wilson and proved popular. As of, say, 1916, the best bet for an envisionable electoral future was probably close competition between the two major

parties indefinitely.[50] But then came act two for the Democrats, the management of World War I and its aftermath,
which seems to have badly damaged them (in Britain, war
management broke up the Liberal party beyond repair)
and brought on their worst defeat ever in 1920. This is contingency. Electorates can key on wars and their aftermaths
just as intently as on domestic concerns. Why shouldn't
that be expected? There is no good reason to credit the
old alleged 1896 realignment for the new postwar Republican hegemony that emerged as—the label is equally warranted—a "System of 1920" that lasted through 1930 and
1932. Note that in both the Clubb, Flanigan, and Zingale
and Bartels calculations, 1920 earns a better license as a
realigning juncture than does 1896, and an appealing
1876-like narrative could be composed about it.[51]

50. It may be objected that the Republicans held a national edge in party
identification during the 1910s and were likely to keep it. The latter, at least,
is just supposition. At any rate, of the twenty-five presidential elections since
1900, how many have produced victories by parties holding national edges
in party identification at the relevant times? Fourteen of them, or 56 percent,
is a reasonable guess. That is small gain over an expectation of 50 percent
through flipping coins. (This calculation assumes a Republican edge in
identification through 1932, a Democratic edge after that. The hardest call is
probably 1932. There is no way to be sure about such edges during the first
third of the century, since recall evidence compiled on the matter in later
voter surveys is problematic.)

51. Sources for such a narrative might include: Wesley M. Bagby, *The
Road to Normalcy: The Presidential Campaign and Election of 1920* (Baltimore: Johns Hopkins University Press, 1962); William E. Leuchtenburg,
The Perils of Prosperity, 1914–1932 (Chicago: University of Chicago Press, 2d
ed., 1993), chs. 4, 5; George Soule, *Prosperity Decade: From War to Depression, 1917–1929* (New York: Rinehart, 1947), chs. 4, 5; David Burner, *The

Second, why should we suppose that the alleged "insulation" came to be *needed* after 1896? (The Schattschneider and Burnham "functional" argument is at issue here.) It hadn't been needed previously: certainly the American business community had done well enough for itself in the relatively uninsulated context of vigorous two-party competition, less accentuated sectionalism, and high (male) voter turnout between the mid-1870s and the mid-1890s. As for the American economy's presumably high-tension "takeoff," that phase had occurred, according to W. W. Rostow's schematization, rather earlier, between 1843 and 1860, under Presidents Tyler through Buchanan.[52]

And insulation from what? A major defect in the Sys-

Politics of Provincialism: The Democratic Party in Transition, 1918–1932 (New York: Knopf, 1968), 43, 72; Arthur S. Link, *American Epoch: A History of the United States Since the 1890's* (New York: Knopf, 1955), ch. 11; Robert K. Murray, *The Harding Era: Warren G. Harding and His Administration* (Minneapolis: University of Minnesota Press, 1969), ch. 3; Gary W. Reichard, "The Aberration of 1920: An Analysis of Harding's Victory in Tennessee," *Journal of Southern History* 36 (1970), 33–49, at 39–40; R. A. Burchell, "Did the Irish and German Voters Desert the Democrats in 1920? A Tentative Statistical Answer," *Journal of American Studies* 6 (1972), 153–64; Charles Sellers, "The Equilibrium Cycle in Two-Party Politics," *Public Opinion Quarterly* 29 (1965), 16–38, at 18; Thomas L. Brunell and Bernard Grofman, "Explaining Divided U.S. Senate Delegations, 1788–1996: A Realignment Approach," *American Political Science Review* 92 (1998), 391–99, at 394–96; Clubb, Flanigan, and Zingale, *Partisan Realignment*, 113.

52. W. W. Rostow, *The Stages of Economic Growth* (New York: Cambridge University Press, 1960), ch. 4. Rostow's interpretation has been contested.

tem of 1896 line of thinking is that it ignores the extraordinary success, at least according to certain relevant indicators, of the American society and economy during the
generations both before and after the mid-1890s. Real per
capita income nearly tripled between 1870 and 1910; life
expectancy rose dramatically.[53] The economy grew at
an estimated average annual rate of 4.3 percent between
1871 and 1913.[54] (Another estimate is 4.3 percent between
the early 1870s and the mid-1890s, and 5.6 percent between the mid-1890s and 1913.)[55] Real wages in manufacturing rose by about 40 percent between 1890 and 1914—
a span including the first two decades of the "System of
1896."[56] It is true that short-term troubles could be severe

53. Stuart Bruchey, *The Wealth of the Nation: An Economic History of the
United States* (New York: Harper and Row, 1988), 67–69. On the U.S. economic record between the Civil War and World War I, see also Sidney Ratner, James H. Soltow, and Richard Sylla, *The Evolution of the American
Economy: Growth, Welfare, and Decision Making* (New York: Basic, 1979),
253, 266–71, 308–9; Robert Higgs, *The Transformation of the American
Economy, 1865–1914: An Essay in Interpretation* (New York: Wiley, 1971),
vii, 18–21, 123.

54. United States Bureau of the Census, *Historical Statistics of the
United States, Colonial Times to 1970* (Washington, D.C.: U.S. Government
Printing Office, 1975), vol. 1, p. 225.

55. D. J. Coppock, "The Causes of the Great Depression, 1873–96," *The
Manchester School of Economic and Social Studies* 29:3 (1961), 205–32, at
227.

56. Albert Rees, *Real Wages in Manufacturing, 1890–1914* (Princeton:
Princeton University Press, 1961), 3–4. Rees's findings are discussed and
embraced in Ratner, Soltow, and Sylla, *The Evolution of the American Economy*, 308–9, and in Douglass C. North, *Growth and Welfare in the American*

during the half century after the Civil War, as in 1893, and
that sectors of the farm and blue-collar populations could
and did suffer, but everything we know about electoral
behavior suggests that indicator readings like those above
bring endorsements to regimes and the parties that manage them.

Not least, in what was still dominantly a country of
farmers, agriculture grew and flourished: "The tremen-
dous increase in land ownership, capital goods, and out-
put in American agriculture between the Civil War and
World War I represented an unparalleled advance in the
economic well-being of millions of Americans engaged in
farming. Measured in terms of the wealth acquired by
farmers who had little or no capital at the beginning of
their careers, a greater number of poor and tenant farmers
became members of the middle class than in any previous
period in American history."[57] Understandably in this context, one firewall against Populism in the 1890s seems
to have been indifference or antipathy to it among a
majority of farmers. Iowa, for example, always an agricul-

Past: A New Economic History (Englewood Cliffs, N.J.: Prentice-Hall, 1974),
153–54. For a long time before Rees's study, owing to an earlier study by the
economist and later U.S. Senator Paul Douglas, it seems to have been conventional wisdom that real wages stagnated during the decades around
1900—a picture of, if not exactly the immiseration of the American working
class, at least its non-nonimmiseration. But Rees's findings superseded
Douglas's.

57. Ratner, Soltow, and Sylla, *The Evolution of the American Economy*,
266–67.

tural showcase, stayed with the Republicans in both 1892 and 1896.[58]

In general, the threatening "mass pressures" of the System of 1896 interpretation seem to have been drawn more from tracts than from reality. Probably the best kind of insulation is a high economic growth rate. In actuality, as of the early twentieth century, the chief mass pressures of relevance to the United States were probably those associated with Europeans trying to immigrate to enjoy the country's economy.

One observation by the proponents of the "System of 1896" is indisputable: in many American states of both North and South, close electoral rivalry between Democrats and Republicans gave way to unbalanced competition or one-party supremacy during the late nineteenth century—at least in voting for president.[59] But what

58. On the farmers in 1896, see Gilbert C. Fite, "Election of 1896," in Arthur M. Schlesinger, Jr. (ed.), *History of American Presidential Elections, 1789–1968*, vol. 2 (New York: McGraw-Hill, 1971), 1787–1825, at 1823. For a discussion of why the limited appeal of Populism should have come as no surprise, see John F. Hughes, "The Jacksonians, the Populists and the Governmental Habit," *Mid-America* 76 (1994), 5–26.

59. For the observation, see Schattschneider, "United States: The Functional Approach to Party Government," 202; Walter Dean Burnham, "The Changing Shape of the American Political Universe," *American Political Science Review* 59 (1965), 7–28, at 26; Burnham, "Party Systems and the Political Process," 300–301; Burnham, "The System of 1896: An Analysis," ch. 5 in Paul Kleppner et al., *The Evolution of American Electoral Systems* (Westport, Conn.: Greenwood, 1981), 181. In one effort to compare party competitiveness at the state level over time, Everett Carll Ladd, Jr., has presented a graph entitled, informatively, "Standard Deviations of Differences of Demo-

should we make of that? Did it help to insulate the American business community from challenge? In Schattschneider's interpretation, "One-party politics tends strongly to vest political power in the hands of people who already have economic power."[60] This resembles Key's well-known claim in *Southern Politics* in 1949 that the "have-nots" tend to fare poorly in American state environments lacking competitive parties.[61]

Yet beginning in the early 1960s, a great deal of cross-state, multivariate probing for any such effects of party competitiveness levels came up largely dry,[62] and the

---

cratic Vote for President by State, from the Party's National Percentage." The graph includes data from 1832 through 1968. Possibly the data for 1892 and 1924 should be discounted, since the Democrats hemorrhaged votes in those years to regionally based third parties that provided the chief competition to the Republicans in many states. (This problem is twice as troublesome for 1924 as for 1892, since the La Follette Progressive share of the vote in 1924 was roughly double that of the Populists in 1892.) At any rate, one pattern on the graph is a nearly monotonic rise in the Democrats' cross-state standard deviation value from 1872, a Reconstruction era juncture when the value hit an all-time low of roughly 3 percent, through the Theodore Roosevelt versus Alton Parker election of 1904, when the value reached an all-time high (excepting 1924) of roughly 20 percent. (The time series broke from its pattern of monotonic rise twice during this 1872–1904 time span—dips of less than 1 percent in 1884 and about 4 percent in 1900.) See Ladd, *American Political Parties: Social Change and Political Response* (New York: Norton, 1970), 177.

60. Schattschneider, "United States: The Functional Approach to Party Government," 202.

61. V. O. Key, Jr., *Southern Politics* (New York: Knopf, 1949), ch. 14.

62. See, e.g., Richard E. Dawson and James A. Robinson, "Inter-Party Competition, Economic Variables, and Welfare Policies in the American

search has been largely abandoned.[63] At the level of state politics, at least, the posited effects do not seem to be there. In hindsight, it seems clear that this old body of theorizing either misread the American-style parties or overestimated their importance. Even in a one-party environment, it has been possible for intraparty factions unfriendly to business interests to assert themselves (as did the semisocialist Nonpartisan League in North Dakota around 1920), or for ambitious populist-minded politicians to appeal to electorates (as did Huey Long in Louisiana), or for labor unions to exercise great influence (as in Rhode Island or Hawaii). At the city level, a lack of Republicans numerous enough to offer decent competition in elections did not prevent New York City from building an eye-catching municipal welfare state during the first two-thirds of the twentieth century, or San Francisco from building a "progressive"-style antibusiness regulatory regime in the 1970s and 1980s.[64] Whatever its

States," *Journal of Politics* 25 (1963), 265–89; Thomas R. Dye, *Politics, Economics, and the Public: Policy Outcomes in the American States* (Chicago: Rand McNally, 1966), ch. 9.

63. Key himself made no mention of his have-nots hypothesis in his later work *American State Politics: An Introduction* (New York: Knopf, 1956). See the discussion in David R. Mayhew, "Why Did V. O. Key Draw Back from His 'Have-Nots' Claim?" 24–38 in Milton C. Cummings, Jr. (ed.), *V. O. Key, Jr. and the Study of American Politics* (Washington, D.C.: American Political Science Association, 1988).

64. See Paul E. Peterson, *City Limits* (University of Chicago Press,

balance of party identifiers, every state or city has a median voter who ordinarily needs to be catered to somehow
in elections to its own government. And so does the country as a whole: irrespective of patterns of party competitiveness in the states or cities, parties or politicians acting
strategically in nationwide elections are likely to cater to
the median American voter. That was as true in 1900 or
1920 as it was in 1880 or 1960.

Did voter turnout plunge as a result of the 1896 realignment?[65] The connecting argument here, for Schattschneider and Burnham, is that voter interest sagged in a
great many states in reaction to their sag in party competi-

1981), ch. 10 ("Is New York a Deviant Case?"); Richard Edward DeLeon, *Left
Coast City: Progressive Politics in San Francisco, 1975–1991* (Lawrence: University Press of Kansas, 1992). On the latter city: "Under progressive leadership, San Francisco has asserted its local autonomy, expanded the public
sphere, politicized and democratized the planning process, spurned the dic-
tates of investor prerogative, severely restricted business use of its urban
space, and inured itself to threats of private-sector disinvestment" (2). San
Francisco has formally nonpartisan elections.

65. For an exchange of views on this question, see Philip E. Converse,
"Change in the American Electorate," ch. 8 in Angus Campbell and Philip E.
Converse (eds.), *The Human Meaning of Social Change* (New York: Russell
Sage, 1972), 263–301; Walter Dean Burnham, "Theory and Voting Research:
Some Reflections on Converse's 'Change in the American Electorate,'" *Amer-
ican Political Science Review* 68 (1974), 1002–23; Philip E. Converse, "Com-
ment on Burnham's 'Theory and Voting Research,'" *American Political Sci-
ence Review* 68 (1974), 1024–27; Jerrold G. Rusk, "Comment: The American
Electoral Universe: Speculation and Evidence," *American Political Science
Review* 68 (1974), 1028–49; Walter Dean Burnham, "Rejoinder to 'Comments' by Philip Converse and Jerrold Rusk," *American Political Science
Review* 68 (1974), 1050–57.

tion.[66] In such circumstances, why bother to vote? That was a valid insight, as can be seen in later cross-sectional scholarship where state-level turnout in presidential elections has indeed proven to vary modestly yet significantly with, among other things, closeness of contest.[67] Still, sagging party competition was far from the only contribution to declining turnout around 1900. Much else of relevance was going on. In the North, a wave of reforms that toughened voter registration requirements and otherwise regulated elections seems to have cut sharply into turnout.[68] To my knowledge, no one has crafted a plausible or coherent argument that those reforms had any causal roots in the 1896 realignment.[69] In the South, the formal process of disfranchising African-American voters (as well as many whites) extended from 1889 through 1908.[70] One stimulus

66. See E. E. Schattschneider, *The Semisovereign People: A Realist's View of Democracy in America* (New York: Holt, Rinehart, and Winston, 1960), 84; Burnham, "The Changing Shape of the American Political Universe," 12, 23, 26.

67. See, e.g., Ron Shachar and Barry Nalebuff, "Follow the Leader: Theory and Evidence on Political Participation," *American Economic Review* 89 (1999), 525–47.

68. See Converse, "Change in the American Electorate," 263–301; Rusk, "Comment: The American Electoral Universe."

69. On this question, Burnham has offered what might be called intimations of a causal link, but that is all. See Walter Dean Burnham, *Critical Elections and the Mainsprings of American Politics* (New York: Norton, 1970), ch. 4; Burnham, "Periodization Schemes and 'Party Systems,'" 280–83.

70. On the disfranchising moves, see J. Morgan Kousser, *The Shaping of*

was the election of 1888, which, by giving the Republicans
full control of the federal government for the first time
since 1874, seems to have stirred the South's Democrats
to preemptive action so as to maintain control of their
states.[71] Mississippi held a pioneering disfranchising convention in 1890. Arkansas, Florida, and Tennessee took
steps before 1894. South Carolina acted in 1895. It seems a
reasonable bet that this impulse would have carried on to
its end—that is, action in all eleven ex-Confederate states—
regardless of whether the depression of 1893 or the
McKinley-Bryan confrontation of 1896 ever took place.

Finally, did a System of 1896 impede the development
of a major socialist party in the United States? The case
may be doubted. As Eric Foner has pointed out, the United
States did possess, after all, in the early twentieth century,
a budding socialist party that "appeared to rival those in

---

*Southern Politics: Suffrage Restriction and the Establishment of the One-Party
South, 1880–1910* (New Haven: Yale University Press, 1974), chs. 5, 6; Jer-
rold G. Rusk and John J. Stucker, "The Effect of the Southern System of
Election Laws on Voting Participation: A Reply to V. O. Key, Jr.," ch. 6 in Joel
H. Silbey, Allan G. Bogue, and William H. Flanigan (eds.), *The History of
American Electoral Behavior* (Princeton: Princeton University Press, 1978);
Michael Perman, *Struggle for Mastery: Disfranchisement in the South, 1888–
1908* (Chapel Hill: University of North Carolina Press, 2001).

71. See Perman, *Struggle for Mastery*, 48–51, 54, 61, 67–69, 75–77. Also,
reports of widespread corruption at the polls in 1888 triggered virtually
immediately the successful nationwide reform wave inaugurating the Australian ballot. When implemented in the South, as in Tennessee and Arkansas around 1890, that reform seems to have contributed to African-
American disfranchisement. See ch. 3, esp. 66–67, concerning Arkansas.

Europe, except the German, in mass support and prospects for future growth. Around 1910, the American Socialist party had elected more officials than its English counterpart." But the American party faltered in enrolling immigrant workers, and once World War I began, "apart from the Russian Bolsheviks, the American was the party that remained most true to socialist principles."[72] That is, it refused to back its own nation's military cause—a politically suicidal stance in the United States of 1917–18.[73] By contrast, consider the nationalistic zeal of the Socialist parties in France and Germany. Again, contingency associated with World War I intrudes. In Britain, absent the turmoil of that war, the Labour party might never have catapulted to competitive status—that is, to becoming one of that country's two major parties.[74] As for whether socialism might have filled Burnham's "large hole in [American] voter participation" of the early twentieth century,[75] that counterfactual question is unanswerable. Yes, it could once confidently be asserted by those watching the twentieth century unfold, but the full experience of that

72. Eric Foner, "Why Is There No Socialism in the United States?" *History Workshop*, no. 17, (Spring 1984), 57–80, at 60, 71–72.

73. For a similar interpretation, see Seymour Martin Lipset and Gary Marks, *It Didn't Happen Here: Why Socialism Failed in the United States* (New York: Norton, 2000), 86–87, 184–92.

74. See David Butler and Donald Stokes, *Political Change in Britain: The Evolution of Electoral Choice* (London: Macmillan, 1974), 166, 172, 174.

75. Burnham, "Party Systems and the Political Process," 301.

century supplied too many competing answers. In various places at various times, widespread voter participation seems also to have aided liberalism, Toryism, nationalism, xenophobia, populism, Christian democracy, Communism, fascism, and racism.

Conclusion

7 I HOPE I HAVE SUCCESSFULLY DEMON-
strated that the claims of the realignments
genre do not hold up well, and that its illuminative power has not proven great. Notably, the
various features said to be associated with realignments or critical elections—the causes, precursors,
defining properties, measures, indicators, concomitants,
consequences, and so forth that I have discussed—do not
line up on the historical calendar the way they should.

Yes, the 1932 election stands out for its durable realigning effects, but no one has come anywhere near establishing 1828, 1860, 1896, and 1932 as an exhaustive set
of elections that share that property. Instead, on the evidence of Clubb, Flanigan, and Zingale and of Bartels,
there is a downward cascade from 1932 through the ranks

of 1880, 1920, 1972, 1948, 1876, 1848, 1912, 1896, 1868, 1964, and 1936—to cite the elections that score relatively high in either of those two studies.[1] The 1860 election merits an asterisked status for its majority-party schism, but so does that of 1912. Yes, the postrealignment 1860s and 1930s stand out for their policy innovations, but so do the Progressive era and the 1960s and 1970s, yet decisively *not* the allegedly postrealignment McKinley era. It is true that the election sequence of 1892–96 brought an overhaul of Democratic party ideology, tumultuous nominating conventions, and above-average coalitional realigning values. But it is also true that the sequence of 1874–80 brought unrivaled voter turnout, an extraconstitutional choice of a president, above-average realigning values, and a policy revolution. The sequence of 1910–12 brought third-party showings unmatched even today since the 1850s, above-average realigning values, and a burst of innovative policy making. The sequence of 1948–52 brought a new policy agenda (civil rights and the Cold War), above-average realigning values as the Solid South crumbled,

1. In this list, notice the prominence of elections that followed, or at least occurred during the closing phases of, wars. Included are 1920 (World War I), 1972 (the Vietnam War), 1948 (World War II), 1848 (the Mexican War), and 1868 (the Civil War). Not too far behind in table 1 and fig. 1 is 1952 (the Korean War). In the Civil War case, the collapse of military occupation of the South shaped the elections of 1876 and 1880. Earlier in American history, before widespread suffrage, the election of 1816 brought a basic coalitional shift as footdragging during the War of 1812 put the Federalist opposition out of business. Wars are destabilizing. Only the Spanish-American War failed to leave a lasting electoral dent.

and, according to Gerring, an ideological break point for the Democratic party as it abandoned Bryanism. A century earlier, the election of 1848 brought a major bolt from a nominating convention, an ex-president (Martin Van Buren) on a third-party ticket, and above-average realigning values for both president and Congress.[2] And so it goes. One or more such markers could be associated with the elections of, say, 1856, 1872, 1892, 1924, or 1964. The claims would be lean for contests like those of 1884, 1908, or 1984. But no one has ever argued that all elections are equal. The question is whether they sort themselves correctly onto the realignments calendar—and they do not.

For a scorecard on the point, see table 7.1, which documents the performance of the realignments genre on the various claims discussed in Chapters 2 through 6—all but the very last one about the historically local System of 1896. Covered is the time span from the 1840s through the 1960s—that is, the terrain of the alleged "big three" realigning episodes of 1860, 1896, and 1932 on which the canon has chiefly hinged. The table addresses particular elections, yet each one should be understood to extend to a penumbra of surrounding elections where plausible custom invites that—the 1896 election, for example, often extends to encompass the midterm of 1894.

2. For the 1848 values, see Jerome M. Clubb, William H. Flanigan, and Nancy H. Zingale, *Partisan Realignment: Voters, Parties, and Government in American History* (Beverly Hills, Calif.: Sage, 1980), 92–97.

Table 7.1. Performance of the Realignment Genre on Claims 1–14

Claim	The Big 3 Are the Top 3[b]	All the Big 3 Have Quite High Values[c]	1860 Stars[a]	1896 Stars	1932 Stars	1876 Stars	1912 Stars	1948 Stars
1. Realignment occurs[d]	no	no	no[e]	yes	yes	yes	yes	yes
2. Cyclical pattern[f]	no	no	no	no	no	no	no	no
3. Long tension buildup	no	no	yes	yes?[g]	no	yes[h]	yes?[i]	no
4. Party ID flags before	no	no?	yes	?	?	?	?	no
5. Turnout peaks	no	no	yes	yes	no	yes	no	no
6. Convention turmoil	no	no	yes	yes	no	no	yes	yes
7. Third parties before	no	yes	yes	yes	yes[j]	yes	no	no
8. New issue cleavage	no	?	yes	yes	?[k]	?	?	yes?[l]
9. Ideological polarization	no	no	yes[m]	yes	no	?[n]	yes	no
10. Nationalized House	no	probably	yes	yes	yes	yes	yes	?
11. Policy innovation	no	no	yes	no	yes	yes	yes	yes?[o]
12. Policy embedding	no	no	yes	no	yes	yes	yes	yes?
13. Redistributive policy	no	no	yes	no	yes	yes	yes?[p]	no
14. The voters speak	no	yes	yes	yes	yes	yes	yes	yes

a The year 1860 exhibits quite high values on a particular claim.

b The years 1860, 1896, and 1932 dominate all other elections.

c The years 1860, 1896, and 1932 all have quite high values, although that may be true of other elections too.

d Data presented by Clubb, Flanigan, and Zingale (CF&Z) or Bartels show quite high readings.

e There is no tall peak in the CF&Z times series, although a party schism did occur, as in 1912.

f Thirty years or so have elapsed since last peak in CF&Z or Bartels data series.

g Agricultural discontent had been rising, albeit inconstantly, in the southern and plains states, yet the depression of 1893 probably accounts for most of what took place in the 1894 and 1896 elections.

h There was a snowballing reaction of southern whites to Appomattox and Reconstruction.

i There was a rise of reform demands associated with Progressivism.

j The association with 1924 with 1932 may be a stretch; it is difficult to say.

k Gerring did not find a new issue cleavage.

l Civil rights may meet the standard.

m Polarization, yes; whether it was ideological is unclear.

n Polarization certainly occurred in the Deep South; otherwise unclear.

o Does Cold War internationalism meet the standard?

p Congress enacted the statutory income tax in 1913, high top-bracket income tax rates in 1916, an inheritance tax in 1916.

Column 2 ("The Big 3 Are the Top 3") poses the stiffest test to the realignments genre: claim by claim, has each of the elections of 1860, 1896, and 1932 dominated every other election from the 1830s through the 1960s? On this reckoning, the genre flunks all fourteen claims. A softer test is "All the Big 3 Have Quite High Values." That is, the elections of 1860, 1896, and 1932 all register, let us say, quite high results on any given claim,[3] regardless of whether any other elections during the century and a half might have registered impressive results also. In fact, on almost all the fourteen claims, one or more of the non-canonical elections have done that.[4] Perhaps surprisingly, the realignments genre scores almost as poorly on this second test as it does on "The Big 3 Are the Top 3." The last six columns present claim-by-claim scores for the three canonical elections as well as three plausible noncanonical rivals—1876, 1912, and 1948. On this last evidence, which is complicatedly checkered, how could a judgment

3. "Quite high" is a matter of judgment for most of the entries in table 7.1. In principle, for any claim, I reached for rankings in roughly the top 30 percent of all elections between the 1830s and the 1960s. That cutoff is, among other things, just generous enough to rate the election of 1896 "quite high" in either the Clubb, Flanigan, and Zingale or the Bartels measure of durable realignment. See table 4.1 and fig. 4.1, this vol.

4. The likely exceptions are claims 2 and 4, on which the canonical elections do not perform all that well either. On claim 13 (redistributive policy), some good candidates for yes scores would be the elections of 1912 (followed by the statutory income tax), 1920 (followed by the Mellon tax cuts), and 1964 (followed by Medicare and the Voting Rights Act). Outside the time span surveyed here is the election of 1980 (followed by the Reagan tax and spending cuts).

arise that the members of the first threesome are different in kind from the members of the second?[5]

In the face of these difficulties, what kinds of generalizations remain available about American electoral history? Are there any? I will conclude by suggesting two alternative lines of thinking. The first line is nominalistic, dissolvent, skeptical; it questions the very idea of constructing anything as grand as realignment theory. In particular, any partitioning of electoral history into regular spans of time is likely to rub up against reality and fail. There is a great deal to be said for this view. Helping it along are three distinct ideas that can be seen as antidotes, so to speak, to the system-building ambition of the realignments genre.

The first is the idea of *contingency*. As I argued earlier, electoral politics, as new events trigger new issues, is to an important degree just one thing after another. To

5. In this book, I have steered clear of examining patterns of congressional roll-call voting for indirect evidence of electoral realignments. If the work of Keith T. Poole and Howard Rosenthal is accepted as a guide to this subject, there is no evidence in it of "realignment interaction," to use the terminology of Clubb, Flanigan, and Zingale for quick, long-lasting cleavage alterations, in the roll-call patterns of either the 1890s or the 1930s. Also drawing on the Clubb, Flanigan, and Zingale terminology, there *is* evidence in Poole and Rosenthal of "realignment surges"—that is, relatively long-lasting shifts of Senate or House member means on a left-to-right roll-call dimension—in the 1890s and 1930s. But those surges are not any more remarkable than the ones of the Progressive era, the 1920s, or the 1940s. See Poole and Rosenthal, *Congress: A Political-Economic History of Roll Call Voting* (New York: Oxford University Press, 1997), chs. 5 and 9, 43n14, 59–60, 73.

the extent that this is true, elections and their underlying causes are not usefully sortable into generation-long spans. A scandal, a fancy, a blunder, a depression, or a world war may come along and swerve voters. A terrorist attack may do that. Any kind of contingency-free theorizing about real politics has serious limitations.

A second idea is *short-term strategy* as it is plied by candidates and parties, both of which tend to cater to the electorate as well as to emanate from it. (The two animations are difficult to disentangle; I am emphasizing the former here.) To the degree that parties and candidates seek election victories above all else, they will tend to converge at the voter median and bring on close elections. That tendency, rather than any "evasion" by the major parties of a hypothetical oncoming wave of populism,[6] probably accounts for the close "Tweedledum versus Tweedledee" elections of the 1880s—not to mention the election of 2000. As argued earlier, such victory strategies carry another implication: parties and candidates may accommodate major impulses from the electorate without any telltale signs of realignment appearing in elections. Consider, for example, the contests of 1940 and 1948. One perhaps surprising result is that the magnitude of voter realignments, however that concept may be defined, cannot

6. As in James L. Sundquist, *Dynamics of the Party System: Alignment and Realignment of Political Parties in the United States* (Washington, D.C.: Brookings Institution, 1973), 92–94, 144, at 144.

come close to indexing the importance, innovativeness, consequentiality, or level of voter concern that underpins elections.

Combine the ideas of contingency and victory-oriented strategy, and certain results reported by Daniel J. Gans in 1985 become understandable. In the sequence of presidential elections from 1856 through 1980, the distribution of victory "runs" by party (Carter, for example, was a run of one for the Democrats; Reagan and Bush a run of three for the Republicans) did not differ significantly from what you would expect to get in runs of heads and tails through coin flips.[7] Also, in the absence of repeat major-party candidates (such as Reagan in 1984, or Bryan in 1900), a presidential election four years ago holds virtually zero predictive value for this year's election—either in predicting this year's victorious party or this year's party shares of the vote.[8]

The third idea is *valence* issues, a concept introduced by Donald J. Stokes in 1966 and given major play, at least implicitly, in the sizable econometrics literature gauging the effects of ups and downs of the economy on elections.[9]

7. Daniel J. Gans, "Persistence of Party Success in American Presidential Elections," *Journal of Interdisciplinary History* 16 (1985), 221–37, at 228–30.

8. Ibid., 230–33.

9. Donald E. Stokes, "Spatial Models of Party Competition," 161–79 in Angus Campbell, Philip E. Converse, Warren E. Miller, and Donald E. Stokes, *Elections and the Political Order* (New York: Wiley, 1966). For econo-

Instead of "position" issues, where one party favors policy
X and the other party favors policy Y—the staple kind
of cleavage in the realignments genre—"valence" issues
hinge chiefly on perceived government management: my
party can manage the economy or the war, for example,
better than your party has been doing. The more one examines American electoral history, the more it seems
to tilt toward valence-issue as opposed to position-issue
junctures. More than it did two generations ago, for example, the electoral turmoil of the 1890s seems to implicate
the depression of 1893 as much as Bryan's insurgency.
Across the Atlantic, that same depression appears to have
elevated the British Tories into the age of Salisbury and
Balfour through an 1895 election just as it elevated the
Republicans into the age of McKinley in 1894 and 1896.[10]
In other American contests, a poor economy figured in the
important midterm of 1874, and, according to one recent

metric analyses using long time series, see Gerald Kramer, "Short-Term
Fluctuations in the U.S. Voting Behavior, 1896–1964," *American Political
Science Review* 65 (1971), 131–43; D. Roderick Kiewiet and Michael Udell,
"Twenty-Five Years after Kramer: An Assessment of Economic Retrospec-
tive Voting Based upon Improved Estimates of Income and Unemploy-
ment," *Economics and Politics* 10 (1998), 219–48.

10. See Henry Pelling, *Popular Politics and Society in Late Victorian
Britain* (London: Macmillan, 1968), 92; Neal Blewett, *The Peers, the Parties
and the People* (London: Macmillan, 1972), 17–19; Michael Kinnear, *The
British Voter: An Atlas and Survey since 1885* (Ithaca: Cornell University
Press, 1968), 24; Paul A. Readman, "The 1895 General Election and Political
Change in Late Victorian Britain," *The Historical Journal* 42 (1999), 467–93,
at 482.

analysis, a quick nationwide economic downturn was a central ingredient in the Whigs' great victory of 1840.[11]

Valence issues, which by their nature exemplify contingency and often bring into play opportunistic candidate or party strategies, are not friendly territory for the realignments genre. For his purposes, Sundquist downplays them on the ground that, in the long run, it is opposing policy positions that anchor voters. "Parties have often been expelled from office by the voters, for example, because of scandal and corruption. . . . But in the main, the voters see every party as harboring both crooks and reformers, and the usual effect of scandal is deviation rather than realignment."[12] As it happens, even this claim is shaky: it is not clear that valence issues should be so dismissively identified with deviation—particularly in the area of economic management. As against Sundquist, one plausible size-up of the parties by canny voters might be: they can put on and take off issue positions like suits of clothes, but a party's incompetence is likely to be deeply embedded.[13] Consider the following successes scored by opposition parties just

11. Michael F. Holt, "The Election of 1840, Voter Mobilization, and the Emergence of the Second American Party System: A Reappraisal of Jacksonian Voting Behavior," 16–58 in William J. Cooper, Jr., Michael F. Holt, and John McCardell (eds.), *A Master's Due: Essays in Honor of David Herbert Donald* (Baton Rouge: Louisiana State University Press, 1985).

12. Sundquist, *Dynamics of the Party System* (1983), 303–4. Sundquist uses the general term *valence issues* in crafting this argument.

13. I owe this idea to Alan Gerber, although I own up to the wording being mine.

after the country's three worst economic downturns: in the wake of 1873, the Democrats captured control of the House and kept it for sixteen of the next twenty years. After 1893, the Republicans captured the House and kept it for sixteen consecutive years. After 1929, the Democrats captured the House and also kept it for sixteen consecutive years. The last of these spans acquired a relevant asterisk, however. After the sharp economic contraction of 1937–38, which was "in terms of speed if not duration . . . the most serious in the nation's history," a cross-party "conservative coalition" rose to a House ascendancy in the 1938 midterm election that lasted for some sixteen years, notwithstanding formal Democratic control of the chamber during most of that time.[14]

It is not a minor matter that contingency, strategy, and valence issues tend to infuse elections. Blindsided by that threesome, for example, were Germany's Social Democrats and Communists in the early 1930s—believing as they tended to do that history would eventually favor their class-based cause and they could just wait.[15] Politics can-

14. Patrick Renshaw, "Was There a Keynesian Economy in the USA between 1933 and 1945?" *Journal of Contemporary History* 34 (1999), 337–64, at 344. On the 1938 midterm, see also David R. Mayhew, "Innovative Midterm Elections," ch. 10 in Philip A. Klinkner (ed.), *Midterm: The Elections of 1994 in Context* (Boulder, Colo.: Westview, 1996), 160–61. The Republicans gained eighty House seats in 1938, a figure unmatched since.

15. On the German Social Democrats, see Sheri Berman, *The Social*

not be about waiting—for electoral realignments or any-thing else. In the real world, voters are called upon to make judgments, not just to register long-term interests or preferences—and to make them all the time. It is a Rip Van Winkle view of democracy that voters come awake only once a generation.

That is the nominalist case against the realignments project. But there is a second line of thinking in response to that project. Suppose we do admit the utility of trying to detect patterns across American political history, or at any rate much of it, in a fashion that draws together elections, parties, and policy innovation. Most of us do that some-how anyway, at least haphazardly. It would be hard not to. Obviously, as with the realignments genre, any effort to detect patterns requires decision rules: How can we be sure we are seeing one? But for purposes here, I would like to bypass that methodological concern to present a large empirical question and then suggest some off-the-top an-swers to it. The question is: If we play fair with the Ameri-can historical record, what will the *content* of any patterns connecting elections, parties, and policy making likely turn out to be? What is the story out there waiting to be told? Is it one story? Is it several stories?

For Schattschneider, Burnham, largely Sundquist, and

Democratic Movement: Ideas and Politics in the Making of Interwar Europe (Cambridge: Harvard University Press, 1998), ch. 8.

often Key, writing from their vantage point in the 1950s and 1960s, that set of questions had a ready answer.[16] Stripped down to its basics, American political history had been a continuing, zero-sum contest between, on the one hand, an acquisitive and domineering business class and, on the other, a chiefly lower-bracket coalition of farmers and laborers bent on curbing those mercantile or capitalist propensities. That had been the theme of the Democrats' countless Jefferson–Jackson Day dinners as well as of, in academic life, the influential school of Progressive historians led by Charles Beard, J. Allen Smith, and V. L. Parrington in the early twentieth century.[17] In this spirit, the junctures of American history worth memorializing had included 1800, 1828, and 1932 with their great victories by respectively the Jeffersonians, the Jack-

16. For the argument of this paragraph, V. O. Key, Jr., is a mixed case. In *Southern Politics in State and Nation* (New York: Knopf, 1949), he of course emphasized a political cleavage based on race, and sometimes in his writings he argued like a straight pluralist, but the Beardian line is there too. Even in *Southern Politics*, the South's racial cleavage comes across as a kind of distraction. A more natural or rational politics of higher versus lower income brackets would have prevailed if race had not intruded; see, e.g., 131, 146, 255.

17. On this subject, see Richard Hofstadter, *The Progressive Historians: Turner, Beard, Parrington* (New York: Knopf, 1969). Burnham explicitly buys into the Progressive historians' line of analysis in Walter Dean Burnham, "The System of 1896: An Analysis," ch. 5 in Paul Kleppner et al., *The Evolution of American Electoral Systems* (Westport, Conn.: Greenwood, 1981), 154. "But the struggle perceived by Beard, Vernon L. Parrington, and others—always latent as an axis of cleavage—comes clearly to the surface when the performance of the economy produces massive dislocations and suffering among the electorate."

sonians, and the New Dealers, and the mid-1890s by virtue of its great tragedy as Populism and the Bryan cause failed. The Civil War era presented problems of fit, but, in accord with the motif of conflict between economic formations, it did at least offer a clash between slave and nonslave modes of production, and in Beard's well-known analysis it was the occasion for the rise of American capitalism to hegemonic standing.

The general picture offered here of American history is one of economic dualism, and with Beard as with Marx, a suitably formulated vision of that sort can have an engaging feature: A "doctrine of progress," to use Richard Hofstadter's phrase, can result.[18] One finds that spirit in Burnham, for whom, notwithstanding the disasters of the 1890s, "it can nevertheless be argued that the sectionalism of the 1896–1932 alignment significantly advanced the nationalization of American politics." The vanquishing of the Democratic party in the northeastern industrial quadrant in the 1890s "bore within it the seeds" of later regeneration. The old Gold Democratic leadership disappeared in the North, but "this vacuum was in time to be filled" by newer leaders. "The stage was thus gradually set" for the styles, alliances, and triumphs of the New Deal era.[19] Through metaphors, a kind of dialectic is being

18. Hofstadter, *The Progressive Historians*, 200.
19. Walter Dean Burnham, "Party Systems and the Political Process," ch. 10 in William Nisbet Chambers and Walter Dean Burnham (eds.), *The*

played out here, although Burnham does not use the term in this passage (he uses it elsewhere).[20]

Unquestionably, the tale developed by the Progressive historians appears in *one* pattern available from the mass of discursive and statistical evidence about American electoral history. The Democrats' surge victory in 1932 had its farmer-labor coalitional aspect; the Populist and Bryan elections of the 1890s were striking on several counts; the 1850s and 1860s were turbulent times; and so forth. Yet, as I hope I have demonstrated, the quest by the re-alignments writers for a one-to-one correspondence—their insistence, in effect, that certain great dates of the economic-dualism story, 1800, 1828, 1860, 1896, and 1932, add up to an exhaustive list of the great dates of American electoral history grounded in actual empirical analysis—will not work. It does not come close to working.

That is at least because other stories can be told. In fact, American electoral history is a common carrier of stories. Let me suggest three others that seem to rival in importance the economic-dualism story, at least as regards long stretches of American history, in drawing together elections, parties, and policy making. In line with my previous arguments about 1940 and 1948, the elec-

---

American Party Systems: Stages of Political Development (New York: Oxford University Press, 1967), 301.

20. Walter Dean Burnham, *Critical Elections and the Mainsprings of American Politics* (New York: Norton, 1970), 27.

tions figuring in these stories have not necessarily exhibited lasting wrenches, or indeed sometimes any wrenches at all, in voter alignments. Instead, conventional historical evidence about what seems to have happened when and why is the guide. Policy themes and an eye for electoral verdicts, irrespective of their statistical properties, are the starting points.

The first story is about *bellicosity*.[21] From the 1750s through the 1860s, not a generation went by without one interest or another risking and provoking war on the North American continent. Five major wars were fought—a set of events reminiscent of state formation in central Europe and as fundamental as anything could be to "American political development."[22] After 1789, elections played a role. Prussia with elections is a fair image. The midterm election of 1810 sent the so-called war hawks to Congress, where they helped trigger the War of 1812, which ended in a burst of American nationalism accompanied by new government policies—the country's first protective tariff and the Second Bank of the United States, both established in 1816. In the election contest of 1844,

21. In these three stories I am emphasizing electoral choice—that is, expressions by the electorate that have arguably left important marks on policy making. That distinguishes this case about bellicosity from an earlier remark that wars have often affected electoral patterns.

22. For the developmental significance of the first of these five conflicts, the French and Indian War, as Americans call it, see Fred Anderson, *Crucible of War: The Seven Years' War and the Fate of Empire in British North America, 1754–1766* (New York: Knopf, 2000).

Democratic party enthusiasts for the annexation of Texas, a move that risked war with Mexico, ended up victorious and the annexation and the war both soon came, engendering in turn an immense additional territorial expansion and a policy debate possibly unrivaled in length and intensity that ended in the Compromise of 1850. And of course in the election contest of 1860, both the northern and southern causes hung tough as civil war, with its many consequences, loomed. Consider this question: Is there a *better* story than this one that would involve elections, parties, and policy making for the first third or so of American national history? In the policy area, the alleged realignment of 1828 does not provide much grist for an alternative story. For one thing, why should the nonrenewal of the Second Bank of the United States in 1832—probably the chief domestic policy innovation of Andrew Jackson's presidency—be considered more remarkable than the establishment of that bank in the first place in 1816?

The second story is about *race*. Ordinarily a more explosive subject than class, race has somehow or other intruded into elections, party strategies, and policy making throughout most of American history. Relevant electoral junctures of the mid-nineteenth century include 1844 with its Liberty Party, 1848 with its Free Soil defection, 1854 with its Republican mobilization in reaction to the Kansas-Nebraska Act, 1860 as a preface to the Civil War, and 1866 as a preface to Reconstruction. There is the showdown politics of the mid-1870s that the realignments canon has paid so little attention to. (Sundquist gives it just a few scattered sentences in his 449-page book.)[23] In the Gilded Age, two midterm elections were conducted *while* Republican Congresses were considering ambitious civil rights bills that drew public attention—in 1874, the Civil Rights Act of 1875 (this was enacted in the lame-duck session after the election but never enforced),[24] and in 1890, the Federal Elections Rights bill (this was defeated in the ensuing lame-duck session).[25] In both cases, the midterm voters overwhelmingly rejected the ruling Republicans. As discussed earlier, these elections had other issues, yet there seems to have been a flavor of racial referendum to both of them. Race issues receded after the Republicans' Indian-summer legislative drive of 1890–91, but of course they surged back to help lend structure to

23. James L. Sundquist, *Dynamics of the Party System: Alignment and Realignment of Political Parties in the United States* (Washington, D.C.: Brookings Institution, 1983). There are passing references at 8, 103–4, 123, and 305.

24. See Michael W. McConnell, "The Forgotten Constitutional Moment," *Constitutional Commentary* 11 (1994), 115–44, at 115. "But [Senator Charles] Sumner's proposed Civil Rights bill was the single most contentious issue in 1874, especially in the South. The bill had passed the Senate in May but was bottled up in the House. It is not too much to say that the election of 1874 was a referendum on the nation's continued commitment to civil rights" (124).

25. This proposed measure was also called the "Force Bill." See Stanley P. Hirshson, *Farewell to the Bloody Shirt* (Bloomington: Indiana University Press, 1962), 200–35; H. Wayne Morgan, *From Hayes to McKinley: National Party Politics, 1877–1896* (Syracuse: Syracuse University Press, 1969), 339–43.

electoral politics after World War II. In 1948, the Democrats' shift to a pro-civil rights stance fractured the Solid
South. The party's civil rights initiatives of the mid-1960s
cemented African-American loyalties but alienated many
whites, a pattern that persists.[26] This narrative is complicated and uneven, but on balance race has probably made
as much of a mark on American electoral history as have
farmer-labor coalitions struggling against merchants and
capitalists.

The third story is about *economic growth*. What can it
mean if year after year, decade after decade, as shown in
econometric analysis, voters tend to reward governments
for rises in per capita income and penalize them for
slumps in that indicator?[27] The pattern is exceptionally
robust—even if other factors must have weighed heavily in
election years such as 1912, 1952, and 1968. What can it
mean if voters behave in this economistic way? This is a
contested subject, yet certainly one plausible hypothesis is
that, in general, governments are likely to react by doing
their best to spur economic growth.[28] Voters in effect ask
for a growth regime, and by inducing the appropriate in-

26. See Edward G. Carmines and James A. Stimson, "On the Structure
and Sequence of Issue Evolution," *American Political Science Review* 80
(1986), 901–20.

27. See, e.g., Kiewiet and Udell, "Twenty-Five Years after Kramer."

28. For an argument like this one, plus an excellent recent treatment of
the relevant econometrics literature, see D. Roderick Kiewiet, "Economic
Retrospective Voting and Incentives for Policymaking," *Electoral Studies* 19
(2000), 427–44.

centives in politicians, they probably tend to get it. That may be the final meaning of historical junctures that juxtapose the economy and the polity like those of 1893–96 and 1929–32. For Democrats who campaigned against Hoover for a generation after 1932, the lesson was obvious. For their part, academics have tended to dismiss campaign slogans of the past like "the full dinner pail" and "a chicken in every pot" on the grounds that something deeper must have been going on in those elections. But perhaps it wasn't. An electoral connection that tends to spur economic growth may be enough. With this kind of analysis, which points to a positive-sum rather than a zero-sum political economy, we see another long-running story about history that draws together elections, parties, and policy making.

Those are general stories, yet individual elections have their stories too. Central to the realignments genre has been the story of 1896. Accordingly, one final test for the genre might be: Did it successfully elevate 1896 to a level with 1860 and 1932? That, one senses, was its chief aspiration—both as science (to wit, the statistics and the alleged periodicity) and as political and historical assertion. The Bryan cause of 1896 was so terribly important, after all. But it was a *losing* cause, if an interesting and important one, and as such it is a member of a large universe of not easily analyzable "roads not taken." History moved on more or less seamlessly, and seamlessness does not easily rival the memorable events of the Civil War and New Deal eras. Between these two eras, if one's particular concern is electoral turbulence—that is, alignment wrenches—at least four junctures catch the eye. The choice of which to dwell on is largely a matter of policy interest. For race and section, there is the election sequence of 1874 through 1880. For center-periphery relations or a last-gasp reaction to industrial capitalism, there is 1892 through 1896. For state building in the Progressive mode, there is 1910 through 1916. For U.S. international involvement and the ricochet from it, there is 1916 through 1920. There is no good scientific or historical reason to award primacy to any of these four.

In closing, where does that leave the realignments perspective in general? There is a possible fallback for it. How about settling for a stripped-down version? Even granted all the criticism elaborated above, even if the 1890s should be abandoned, why not keep using the term *realignment* to characterize the two genuine outlier eras of American political history—the 1860s and 1930s? That would justify the generality of the term. Also, why not keep writing about gradual, or secular, realignments? Journalists are certain to go on using the term *realignment* anyway. Why shouldn't political scientists?

The problem is that, for professional political scientists, the benefits of this course are small and the costs are significant. Obviously, gradual electoral change is worth studying in its own right. Half a century ago, for example, South Carolina was possibly the most Democratic state in the country, and Vermont the most Republican. Today nearly the reverse is true. This kind of drift cries out for attention. But at today's stage of scholarship, no conceptual or theoretical utility is added by use of the terms *secular* or *realignment.*

In the case of the 1860s and 1930s, probably all the utility that can be wrung from the electoral realignments analogy has already been wrung. The analogy has limits, after all. The turmoil centering in the 1860s featured the collapse of a major party, extreme polarization, capture of the presidency by a party winning 39.9 percent of the vote (the Republicans under Lincoln), ambitious policy ventures that could hardly lose in an environment where an eleven-state interest had vacated Capitol Hill (imagine the policy results in today's Congress if, say, all the members from northeast of West Virginia stayed home), a civil war that cost six hundred thousand lives, and military occupation of a sizable part of the country. Nothing like any of these developments occurred in the 1930s. For analytic purposes, it might make sense to bypass the analogy between the 1860s and the 1930s and ask instead a cross-national question: How do civil wars intersect with elections? Is there a trademark breakdown dynamic? Are party identifications distinctively hardened by civil wars? The universe of at least partly relevant instances is small but it exists—for example, Switzerland in the 1840s, Ireland and Finland at the close of World War I, Spain in the 1930s, and Greece after World War II.

By contrast, the American elections of the 1930s brought principally, albeit not only, a lasting voter "surge." For analytic purposes, what are we to make of that? Again, cross-national comparisons might be useful. One way to try to get a handle on America of the 1930s—plus the 1890s, the 1870s, and possibly even earlier junctures, such as 1840—is to look into depression-induced voter surges in general. In Britain, for example, the depressions of *both* 1893 and 1929 seem to have helped Tory-centered coalitions to lasting power, through the elections of 1895 and 1931. In Canada, a newly dominant Liberal Party helped to power by the poor economic times of the 1890s ruled for virtually the same time span—1896 through 1911— as America's Republicans of the McKinley era.[29] In Europe, the depression of 1929 aided, among other parties, Sweden's Socialists and Germany's Nazis. Beyond depressions, there is a case for cross-national comparison of voter surges triggered by international, as opposed to civil, wars. In this regard, the United States after World War I resembled Britain but also Australia. In all three

29. J. Bartlett Brebner, *Canada: A Modern History* (Ann Arbor: University of Michigan Press, 1960), chs. 21, 22, 24.

countries, center-left governments seem to have paid a heavy price for war management.[30]

In short, even stripped back to its secular connotation or its analogy between the 1860s and the 1930s, the realignments way of thinking adds little or no illumination, but it does exact opportunity costs. Other lines of investigation might be more promising. Yet there is another problem. Could the realignments perspective really be stripped back? Could the ideas about cycles, periodicity, party systems, and the System of 1896—all the ingredients of what I have called the fully fleshed-out version of the realignments perspective—really be struck from everyone's mental agenda if the realignments metaphor should carry on? That is doubtful. And that supplies a good argument for abandoning the terminology entirely. The ambitious version of the realignments perspective had its fruitful days, but it is too slippery, too binary, too apocalyptic, and it has come to be too much of a dead end.

---

30. On Australia: "It is evident that wartime strains completed a realignment of Australian politics. The Labor Party, having lost power at the end of 1916, would not regain it for more than a decade—and then only briefly—and would fail to command a majority in both houses of the Commonwealth parliament until 1944. The conservatives . . . would hold the initiative for a full quarter-century." Stuart MacIntyre, *The Oxford History of Australia*, vol. 4, *1901–1942: The Succeeding Age* (New York: Oxford University Press, 1986), 190.

Index

Ackerman, Bruce, 38n7, 55n17, 118n36
agriculture policy, 23, 62, 107, 114, 120, 121
Aldrich, John H., 4n4, 38–39, 42n15
Australia, 164–65

banking and currency policy: in *1860s*, 104, 115; in
    1890s, 25, 54, 105, 108; Hamilton's, 116; New
    Deal, 114, 120; Second Bank, 157, 158
Bartels, Larry M., 41n11, 50–59, 63n32, 67, 129, 141,
    146n3
Beard, Charles, 154, 155
Beck, Paul A.: on conventions, 74; on cycles, 3, 16, 18–
    20, 36, 65n34, 67–68; on third parties, 22, 78–80
bellicosity, 157–58
Blumenthal, Sidney, 37
Brady, David W., 3, 4n4, 24, 26–27, 100–101, 103–
    108
Britain, 126, 129, 139, 150, 164–65
Bryan, William J., 18, 46n4, 87–90, 143, 161
Burnham, Walter D.: on *2000*, 2n1; on conventions,

The study of electoral realignments is one of the most influential and intellectually stimulating enterprises undertaken by American political scientists. Realignment theory has been seen as a science able to predict changes, and generations of students, journalists, pundits, and political scientists have been trained to be on the lookout for "signs" of new electoral realignments. Now a major political scientist argues that the essential claims of realignment theory are wrong—that American elections, parties, and policy making are not (and never were) reconfigured according to the realignment calendar.

David Mayhew examines fifteen key empirical claims of realignment theory in detail and shows us why each in turn does not hold up under scrutiny. It is time, he insists, to open the field to new ideas. We might, for example, adopt a more nominalistic, skeptical way of thinking about American elections that highlights contingency, short-term election

1924